914.271 W
Wright, G. Walter.
From corncrake to combine
30049003057180

JUL 2015

P9-CFJ-615

DISCARD

From Corncrake
to Combine

FLESH PUBLIC LIBRARY
Piqua, Ohio

DONATED BY

VIOLET DAS

2008

From Corncrake to Combine

Memoirs of a Cheshire Farmer

G Walter Wright

G. WALTER WRIGHT

Edited by Ruth A. Symes

FOREWORD BY MARTIN BELL

914.271 W
Wright, G. Walter.
From corncrake to combine
30049003057180

Piqua Public Library
116 West High Street
Piqua, Ohio 45356

TEMPUS

To my mother and father, for their inspiration

First published 2008

Reprinted 2008

Tempus Publishing
Cirencester Road, Chalford,
Stroud, Gloucestershire, GL6 8PE
www.thehistorypress.co.uk

Tempus Publishing is an imprint of NPI Media Group

© G. Walter Wright, 2008

The right of G. Walter Wright to be identified as the Author
of this work has been asserted in accordance with the
Copyrights, Designs and Patents Act 1988.

All rights reserved. No part of this book may be reprinted
or reproduced or utilised in any form or by any electronic,
mechanical or other means, now known or hereafter invented,
including photocopying and recording, or in any information
storage or retrieval system, without the permission in writing
from the Publishers.

British Library Cataloguing in Publication Data.
A catalogue record for this book is available from the British Library.

ISBN 978 0 7524 4653 0

Typesetting and origination by Tempus Publishing
Printed and bound in Great Britain

Contents

JUL 2015

Acknowledgements

Many people have helped me in the preparation of this manuscript. My sincere thanks go to Greg Barlow for locating the whereabouts of the traction engine 'Winnie' and for providing the photograph of the engine *King George V*; Kathleen Barlow for providing some of the early and wartime photographs; Martin Bell for kindly agreeing to write the preface; Anthony Bloor for his photograph of Mrs Blake and Mrs Bowker picking potatoes; Cheshire and Chester Archives and Local Studies for kind permission to reproduce the photographs of Tatton Hall and King Street, Knutsford; Charles Foster for general advice on publishing; Frank Marshall and Co. for permission to take photographs of Chelford Agricultural Centre; Ron Dickinson for some photography; John Hankey for information on Henry Wilkinson; John Lea (Cranage) for information leading to location of the wartime photograph of Winnie the traction engine; John Lea (Gawsworth) for general advice on publishing; Frank Lythgoe for information on the whereabouts of Winnie the traction engine (now owned by him); Philip Moston (present driver of Winnie) for the recent photograph of the traction engine; Sheila Norbury for the photograph of herself as a land girl; and Hilda Pimlott for information leading to the location of old photographs.

Thanks also to Dr Ruth A. Symes for editing the manuscript; Lorna Tyson for general support of the project and particularly for her memories of her father Bill Davies; Philip Watts for reading some of the early chapters; Roger West, editor of the National Traction Engine Trust's magazine, *Steaming*, for permission to reproduce the photograph of Winnie outside the Kilton Inn; Vera Whittaker for general support and memories of her husband Ted; Mollie Woodbine for her consistent and enthusiastic support of the work, her avid questions and for introducing me to my editor; Barbara Wright for her initial work in typing up the first few chapters; Fiona Wright for her assistance with photographs and photocopies; my wife, Kathleen Wright, for her general support and patience and for helping me to sort out our archive of family photos; Molly Wright for supplying the photographs of High Legh; my son, John Wright, for his photography; and Lieutenant Ted Wurm of the US Army Air Corps for the photograph of Winnie outside the Kilton Inn.

Preface

By Martin Bell OBE

I have written recently of the dismay that I felt on becoming a Member of Parliament. But that was confined entirely to my experiences in the House of Commons, not at all to those in the constituency. During my four years as MP for Tatton, from 1997 to 2001, I was kept going by the knowledge that I represented some truly remarkable people.

Walter Wright was one of them. As soon as I met him, during the rather colourful campaign of April 1997, I realised that here was a man whose vote it would be a privilege to seek: farmer, councillor and all round one-of-a-kind character. If Walter didn't know something, then in all probability it was not worth knowing. He was also a repository of wisdom and folklore, with so special a way of expressing his opinions and experiences, that I hoped one day he would write them all down for the benefit of the rest of us.

And now he has. His book perfectly expresses his character and the love of his life and surroundings – but also the wit of a man who can look in the mirror and sometimes be amused by what he sees. The story of his courtship of Kathleen is typical. it says a lot about both of them that he managed to win her over while afflicted with an unromantic skin condition on the side of his face, the result of spending too much time in the company of heifers. His reminiscences of Cheshire at war are equally intriguing, when the skies were thick with parachutists practising over Tatton Park; and German POWs impressed Cheshire farmers by their hard work in the fields. ('I often wondered how the British Tommy was faring working on German farms. Had he the same enthusiasm?')

From time to time, Walter ventures a few sharp remarks about politicians. What he is too self-effacing to add, is that he is a sort of politician himself, and a consummate one at that – so effective and valued as a local councillor that he was very seldom opposed for re-election. And I still don't know whether I got his vote. But I hope I did.

I feel a special affinity for this country chronicle because it reminds me of my father's first book *Corduroy*, now about to be back in print. Adrian Bell was a generation ahead of Walter Wright, but he too wrote about the changing face of agriculture, the eccentric characters and the engaging oddities of the world around him when he was an apprentice farmer. His work belongs to the literature and history of farming, in the last years when it was done by the unaided muscle power of men and horses (with the exception of the steam-driven threshing machines moving from farm to farm after the harvest).

Walter takes the story on, describing the changes that he sees around him, and by no means approving of all of them. In those days *Cheshire Life* was more than a magazine! We are lucky to have him – and luckier still that he has written it all down.

ONE

Earliest Memories

In my earliest memory, Blossom, our shire horse, lengthens her stride whilst I sit with Father on the lorry riding home from Knowles Pitt Farm to Yew Tree Farm in Mere, North Cheshire. To me, even today, a draught horse starting off a heavily loaded lorry – all will-power and rippling muscles – is a far more impressive show of strength than any other. At the time of my memory, I was just two years old and the year must have been 1933. As our horse and lorry passed Home Farm at Mere Corner, there was a loud squealing noise. I asked Father what it was. 'A pig being killed,' he said in a matter-of-fact way. I looked through the gate across the yard and saw the pig lying on a bench under the archway of the buildings. Even at that tender age, I knew that this was country life – something you just accepted.

I was born in 1931 at Yew Tree Farm, Mere. The farm took its name from a tree in the garden that was about 4ft in diameter and was probably about a thousand years old. The house itself dated back to the sixteenth century – a prosperous time when many farms in the area were built – and it was made to last. There was evidence of a timber frame and wattle and daub walls which had probably been thatched to the ground at some point. A farm building built of bricks (three deep to the first floor and very sturdy) had been added to the house at some point. My world as a small boy was a world of buildings like these: farms and smithies, shippons and barns. My associates and playmates were the characters who lived and worked in them.

Perhaps the most important aspect of Yew Tree Farm was (and continues to be) its location. It lies on the A50 road between two towns: Warrington (seven miles away) and Knutsford (four miles away). In a larger sense, it is exactly half way between the big urban conurbations of Liverpool and Manchester. That road and everything that happened on it has set the tone of my life. It is an important line of communication between all the local markets, but it is also a dangerous place with the traffic along it often travelling too fast and negotiating the bends with difficulty. All too frequently, cars and lorries have landed in our fields: in fact, the famous yew tree itself was demolished by a car that came off the road about twelve years ago.

Family Roots

My mother's maiden name was Alice May Hulme. She was the eldest girl in a family of eleven children who originally lived at Silent Valley Farm, High Legh before they moved in the mid-1920s to Old Farm, High Legh. Prior to her marriage, Mother had been the 'children's help' or nanny for the Dunkerleys – a family who might be described as country gentry – who lived in Meadowlands, a large house nearby. Mother not only lived with the children – Eric, Arthur, Donald and Mary – but also went away on holiday with the family and even had her own passport. By the time my mother met my father, her job with the Dunkerleys was coming to an end. Eric was soon to be married, Arthur was a doctor, Donald was in the Navy and Mary, the youngest child, was also growing up. The Dunkerleys owned three farms in the area:

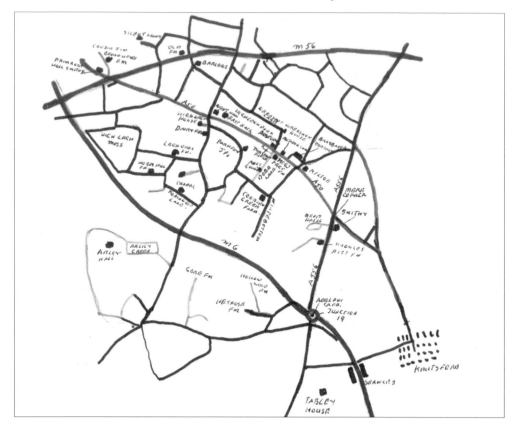

My world: the area in the immediate vicinity of Yew Tree Farm, Mere, North Cheshire.

Before mechanisation: my earliest memories of the farm involve our shire horses, 1930s.

The Cheshire landscape was tamed by the power of men and horses.

Yew Tree Farm before I was born, *c.* 1926.

To the right of the central chimney stack is Silent Valley Farm. Mother's parents lived in one of these two cottages at one point. The building to the left of the chimney stack is the new extension.

Bowdon View Farm (rented by the Masons), Holly House Farm (rented by the Percivals) and Yew Tree Farm - between Meadowlands and the post office – which became ours.

My father's family were local farmers and, at the time of his marriage in 1926, my father and his brother Edmund were tenant farmers at Legh Oaks Farm in High Legh. The previous tenant at Yew Tree Farm was moving on and Father decided to take it on. Mr Dunkerley kindly upgraded the farm especially for my parents, modernising the house with a hot and cold water system including a bathroom and flush toilet. This was Mother's wedding present. Because of the increased traffic on the road at that time, the old barn that jutted out on to the A50 was demolished. Until then, when the threshing machine came along, passing cars had had to negotiate not only the barn but also the baler which often stuck out onto the road. Sometimes they had also had to swerve to avoid the man who was carrying the bales away. The new barn was in a much safer position. It consisted of a stable and loose box with a loft above, a cart shed, a utility room with a fireplace and boiler for when the pigs were killed, and, of course, an outhouse or privy. A four bay Dutch barn was also erected for the storage of corn and hay. This was 1926, at the height of the Depression, but Mr Dunkerley continued – as he had always done – to be a wonderful benefactor for the area. As well as helping those who had worked for his family, such as my mother, he would always find work for the local unemployed setting them the tasks such as grubbing out old hedges and planting trees.

Whilst South Cheshire is a pure dairy area and Lancashire an arable area, the area of North Cheshire in which Yew Tree Farm is situated has traditionally been an area of 'mixed farming'. In the late 1920s and '30s, like many other farmers in the neighbourhood, Father kept cows and hens, and grew oats, wheat and potatoes. At this time, there were no big profits to be made and in some parts of the country agricultural activity was known as 'dog and stick farming'. Father practised rotation cropping; fields that had been grass for three years would be ploughed up so that potatoes or oats could be planted. The following year, Father would plant wheat and the year after that he would plant oats under-sown with grass. This method, dating back centuries, helped

Meadowlands – home of the local landowners, the Dunkerleys.

to combat pests and diseases. A lot of Father's time was spent dealing with the potatoes that made up about 10 per cent of the farm acreage. The seed potatoes would be stored in the lofts above the cattle sheds in winter and left to sprout; in the spring they would be planted outside under manure collected from the cattle.

Technology Comes to Yew Tree Farm

In the early 1930s everything was changing. It was, for instance, the era of early radio. According to Father, when they first married, Mother used to 'listen in' with a crystal and a cat's whisker. They only had one set of headphones and she always fell asleep wearing them. Getting our first proper wireless in about 1935 was a real event. At the same time, we also got piped water and electricity. The water has been coming down the same pipes and the electricity down the same wires at Yew Tree Farm since the early 1930s.

My sister Joyce was born in 1928, and three years later I arrived. We certainly didn't want for relations. The household of my mother's family just a few miles away, at Old Farm, consisted of Grandad (Papa), Grandma and those of their eleven children still remaining at home: Uncles Frank and Charlie, and Aunties Bertha and Gerty. Uncle Frank had taken on the tenancy of Old Farm, Uncle Charlie helped him and Auntie Bertha was the housekeeper who looked after everybody. Auntie Gerty was the youngest member of the family still at home. People regarded her as being a bit 'choosy' because, despite having many admirers, she was still single. Unlike the others, Auntie Gerty had furthered her schooling and had a good job with the Local Education Authority.

When I was young, my mother's two eldest brothers, Arthur and Percy, were already farming elsewhere in Cheshire and I saw them rarely. And, there were two of my mother's siblings whom I never met. One of these was a sister, Mary, who died in 1917 aged ten. I have diaries for 1917 and 1918 written by mother, which (as well as giving a lot of history of the family and local people in the last years of the First World War), also describe how Mary had to go into hospital for an operation, from which she unfortunately never recovered.

The second member of the family whom I never met was Uncle Willie. He went to Canada in 1919 to farm on the prairies and never made the trip home. So far – if you include Mother – I have accounted for nine of the eleven Hulme children. The two remaining brothers, Uncle John and Uncle Joe, also emigrated to Canada; Uncle John in about 1910 and Uncle Joe sometime in the 1920s. I met them much later when they paid visits back to Cheshire in the 1950s and 1960s. These uncles were a source of fascination to me. By all accounts, it was a lonely life on a prairie farm and not many married. The only consolation for Uncle John, I was told, was that he owned a Model T Ford and used to drive into town in it on a Saturday night. Many of the prairie farmers living on their own fared the same way. Uncle Willie remained a bachelor and his last years were spent in an institution looking after the milking herd near to Brandon, Manitoba. Uncle Joe lived a few hundred miles away from him at Swan River and went to visit him occasionally. He said that his brother was happy enough, but Mother was never convinced. She was a great letter writer and the one who liked to keep in touch with all the family. With five brothers in the Army or in Canada at various times, her skills were, no doubt, much appreciated.

Mother liked to see the family at Old Farm as much as possible. Once we got our car in 1935, she insisted that she went to see them at High Legh every Saturday night. Every time we went, the scene was the same: Grandma sitting in her rocking chair and Papa sitting in a quarter chair in the corner next to a Fletcher Russell black kitchen range, smoking his pipe. Auntie Gerty, nick-named 'the Fido' by Uncle Frank, usually wasn't there. She had probably gone to the Lymm picturehouse with her friend Deborah Barlow from the next farm.

Old Farm, High Legh, to which my grandparents moved before I was born. From left to right: Grandpa Hulme, Auntie Gerty and Grandma Hulme, *c.* 1928.

Before my time: Mother's brother Arthur Hulme outside the Jolly Thresher pub, Broom Edge, Lymm, in 1914. The cart is empty, probably indicating that he had just returned from Manchester after delivering a load of hay or straw.

Papa always had the radio on, and would be listening to *In Town Tonight* and then, later in the evening, to *Henry Hall Guest Night*. My sister Joyce and myself, nicknamed 'The Little Wench' and 'Bab', had to keep quiet whilst these shows were on. But, after a while, if I was good, I knew that I could have my interaction with my favourite uncle – Charlie.

Getting About

Before we had a motorcar getting about was a bit difficult. Walking (or 'Shank's Pony' as it was called), or a bicycle were the normal methods of transport. A seat could be fixed on the carrier on the back of a bicycle for a child. We never had a horse and trap. Father must have made a conscious decision about that as he gave Mother a bicycle for a wedding present. I remember occasionally travelling on the bus going to Warrington. The conductor (whose name was Dean but who was affectionately known as 'Dixie' after the footballer), let us use his ticket machine. He knew everybody on the bus.

After we had started to milk our cows twice a day, our time became more precious. We were very grateful when we got our first car – a Morris 8 – in 1935. It was wonderful. With the car, our social life improved no end, and on wet days, we were even taken to school.

Uncle Charlie

Mother's brother Charlie was wonderful with children. I remember sitting on his knee whilst he bounced me up and down with a smile on his face. He had one tooth on a dental plate that he would occasionally drop down. This fascinated me. I couldn't say 'Charlie', so I called him 'Char'. Every Saturday night, it was 'Do it again Char.' Afterwards he would change into his best clothes, say goodbye and go out. I was never told where he was going and I never asked. In later years I was informed that he had been going for his 'health salts' – and I later worked out that these were probably his lady friends. Everybody liked Uncle Charlie, even his old headmaster who called him 'Wag Hulme' because he used to play truant so often. Uncle Charlie had a motorbike, but one lady apparently reckoned you shouldn't go out with Charlie Hulme unless it was on a bus route. He was likely to take off with another woman and leave you stranded, so you needed to make sure you had another method of getting home! When I got my first little cycle I loved going down to Old Farm to visit my grandparents and uncles and aunts. I loved them all, but I would always be looking out for Uncle Charlie in particular.

Uncle Charlie was an expert thatcher. There was no Dutch barn at Old Farm, so the corn sheaves were stacked outside. Stacking was a very skilled job and, to ensure that they lasted throughout the coming year, the stacks needed to be thatched. I remember my Father asking Uncle Charlie to thatch one of our stacks at Yew Tree Farm. He used wheat straw which needed to be cut when it was under-ripe so there was more stiffness and strength in it. We threshed the straw for thatching by hand so that it wasn't as damaged as it might have been if it had gone through a threshing machine. I remember one harvest time when I was quite young, I had bundled up the loose straw round the stack yard into small sheaves and built my own small stack. No doubt I was copying Uncle Charlie. I suppose it must have been talked about in the family and it was agreed that, like the big stacks, my little one needed to be thatched. Uncle Charlie knew that to thatch a stack you required a ladder and it was not long before he came up on his motorbike with a small one especially for my needs.

At that time, a farming paper, *Farming and Stockbreeder*, regularly published pictures of thatchers' work around the British Isles. I was only young at the time, but I could tell that

Uncle Charlie feeding the hens near the stacks he had thatched, 1930s.

Uncle Charlie's expertise was equal to the work of any of the farmers in the magazine. He was an artist.

I had some wonderful times with Uncle Charlie. Like all young country boys, I used to love shooting rabbits and going fishing with my friends. We all had catapults until we were old enough for our first airgun: then we had 4.10 shotguns. Uncle Charlie used to join us boys on rabbiting days in the winter. Sometimes we used ferrets to hunt out the rabbits. I remember once going on a fishing trip with my friend John Wardell and Uncle Charlie to Moss's Pond in the Bent field. Unfortunately, the fishing was not very successful. We didn't miss Uncle Charlie until suddenly there was a loud thrashing noise behind a thorn bush on the side of the pond. There was no chance of catching fish with that racket going on so we put down our rods. To our surprise, Uncle Charlie suddenly swam into view. It was a lovely warm afternoon so it took very little for him to persuade us to jump in and join him in the water. The fact that neither of us had any idea how to swim didn't seem to matter. We had a lovely afternoon frolicking about in the water in our birthday suits. Unfortunately, however, there must have been a sharp object in the mud at the bottom of the pond and, before long, I had cut my ankle rather deeply.

Back at Old Farm, Auntie Bertha bandaged me up without realising how the accident had occurred. While this was happening, Uncle Charlie must have put his wet trunks out to dry from an open window. When Auntie Bertha saw them, she put two and two together and realised that we had all been swimming in the pond. She went berserk. Despite the pain in my ankle, I got on my cycle and went home. My reception there was as I expected: sympathy for my wound but a severe dressing down for going in the pond. Mother reminded me in no uncertain terms of a recent tragic accident when the local policeman was drowned whilst supervising his son fishing. The boy's fishing line had become entangled in the branches of an overhanging tree. The policeman climbed out along a branch to release the line, and when the branch broke, he plunged into the water and drowned. After this experience, my fishing excursions were severely restricted.

Uncle Charlie's thatching talents were second to none, 1930s.

Tragedy at Old Farm

Unfortunately my happy, carefree days with Uncle Charlie were about to end in dramatic fashion. One Sunday morning I went down to Old Farm on my bicycle. As I rode into the yard, Auntie Bertha met me and told me there had been an accident and that I must go home. I could see an ambulance in the field but I rode home without really knowing what had happened. Later I found out. Local contractor Harry Jones had come with his tractor and binder the day before – a Saturday – to cut a field of oats. The dew had come down so he couldn't finish the job, and he had come to finish it that morning.

The corn was always full of rabbits, especially when it was under-sown with grass and clover. Uncle Charlie knew this and, when he went out to help Harry that Sunday morning, he took the shotgun with him on the binder hoping to have some sport. By some means the gun slipped. It was a hammer gun and one of the hammers must have caught. The gun discharged and the shot hit Uncle Charlie, causing severe damage under his arm. Harry Jones did his best to help but, even though blood transfusions were becoming more common at that time, they were not enough to save Uncle Charlie and he died in hospital that night. He was just thirty-one.

The strangest thing about the whole episode was that the Hulmes had never worked in the fields or used a shotgun on a Sunday before. Apparently, Auntie Bertha had questioned Uncle Charlie about whether or not it was right to work on the Sabbath as he took the gun down from its hooks on a beam in the kitchen, but he had just said: 'Better the day, better the deed'. Uncle Charlie's death was a tragic loss, not only to the family, but also to the whole area.

Mere Corner

In my childhood, Mere Corner – the junction of the A556 and the A50 - was reckoned to be one of the busiest crossroads in the British Isles, and was even compared to Hyde Park Corner. The A556 was the main route from Manchester to Chester and consequently very busy. In 1928, shortly before I was born, some of the local farmers had helped to widen the road to four lanes and refurbish the Corner. Old cottages were demolished and new houses, including a post office, were built. The area became known as 'Mere Town.' Local men like Harry Whittaker, Harry Bloor and Joe Whittaker (from Knowles Pitt Farm) worked for a while as labourers on the Corner. This was very welcome work for them. These were hard times and labouring on the roads at least provided a secure income from Cheshire County Council.

The corner boasted the latest technology in the form of traffic lights, but nevertheless, it was the scene of a few accidents over the years. Our neighbour Joe Whittaker wasn't colour blind but he always rode his bicycle – usually with a scythe over his shoulder – straight through those lights. Alas, riding the bicycle was to prove his downfall – literally. One day, he was involved in a fatal accident delivering cabbages to a local hotel.

Local Characters

Whilst my family were the most significant people in my childhood, my early years were also greatly enriched by a gallery of characters from in and around the neighbourhood of Yew Tree Farm.

A POPULAR PERSONALITY

Mr. Charles Hulme's death occasioned widespread regret in High Legh and district, for apart from tragic circumstances Mr. Hulme was a popular personality among the social life and farming community of High Legh.

He was a regular attender at St. John's Church, and for many years was associated with the Private Chapel, being a member of the choir there up to the time the chapel was closed, in 1935. His chief recreation was bowls, at which game he excelled, and was a good "sport." He was also a member of the High Legh Young Men's Club, and of the Auxiliary Fire Service.

The funeral took place at St. Mary's Church, Rostherne, on Wednesday afternoon, where a large number of his relatives and friends assembled. The Rev. J. Oliver (vicar of High Legh) officiated.

The mourners included Messrs. Arthur, Percy and Frank Hulme (brothers); Mrs. Walter Wright and Miss G. Hulme (sisters), Mr. W. Wright (brother-in-law), Mrs. R. Bollington (aunt), Mr. J. Hulme (uncle), Mrs. C. Pickford, Mrs. W. Bostock, Miss M. Wright, Mrs. J. Knowles, Mr. and Mrs. James Wardell, Misses E. M. Wright and J. Knowles, Mrs. A. Bostock, Messrs. James Wright, sen., J. R. Hulme, A. Bostock, James Wright, jun., A. Davies (cousins); Miss A. Davies, Miss Mary Wright, Messrs. John and Tom Wright (Yew Tree Hall), Mr. and Mr. F. J. Gleave, Miss E. S. Wright, Mr. and Mrs. Edmund Wright, Mr. W. H. Winstanley, Mr. T. H. Jones, Mr. Harry Jones (Cherry Lane), Misses L. and D. Barlow, Mr. Harry Percival, Mr. and Mrs. John Wardell, Mr. R. Brookes, Mr. R. Faulkner, Mr. R. Owen (representing Mr. Cornwall Legh), Mr. C. Plumb, Mr. A. Stelfox, Miss K. Cook, Mr. and Mrs. Dennis Cook, Mr. Frank Wright, Mr. J. H. Wright (Cross Roads), Mr. A. R. Cragg, Mr. and Mrs. S. Brookes, Mr. Dowling, Mr. C. Gibbon, Mr. S. Moss, Mr. F. Barlow, Miss Blease and others. Mr. A. R. Cragg and Mr. F. J. Gleave represented the Young Men's Club.

Bearers were Messrs. J. R. Hulme, S. Moss, C. Gibbon, F. Barlow, A. Bostock and James Wright, jun.

LIST OF WREATHS

Wreaths were sent by the following:—All at Home: Percy, Laura and Betty; May and Walter; Jim, Eileen and Winnie; Joyce and Walter; Cousins Jim, Annie and Mary; Aunt Louie and Uncle Robert; Cousins Jessie and Gertie; Bertha and Willie; Mary and John; Jim and Lois; Herbert and Joe and families; Arthur, Clara and Kathleen; Cousins at Clarke Lane; All at Legh Oaks; Mr. and Mrs. F. Wardell and family; John; Mr. and Mrs. John Wardell and Kenneth; Kay Lane Farm; Ced. and family; Miss Surridge; Mr. and Mrs. S. Moss; Mr. and Mrs. Cornwall Legh; Men's Club; Mr. and Mrs. Barlow and family; Mr. and Mrs. J. H. Jones and family; Dennis and Mary; Mr. and Mrs. Brookes and family; Mr. and Mrs. Faulkner; Charlie and all at Moss View; Kathleen Cook; Mr. and Mrs. William Cook; Arthur, Susie and family; Nurse; All at Little Heath Farm; Mr. and Mrs. J. Lomax and family; Alice, Edna and Lilian (Broomedge); Mr. and Mrs. Canning and Nancy; Mr. and Mrs. T. Jones; Mr. and Mrs. T. Williams; Mr. and Mrs. Stephen Haworth; Mr. and Mrs. Hazledene and family; Mr and Mrs. Jocelyn Walker and family.

The report in the *Manchester Guardian* of Uncle Charlie's untimely death in 1940.

The Deans – An Enterprising Couple

In the lodge next to Meadowlands lived a man whom my sister Joyce and I used to call 'Mr Oogly Googly'. This was because he often used to look at us in our pram, wave his finger round in a circle and say, 'Oogly googly'. His real name was Ted Dean and he was the chauffeur and gardener for the Dunkerley family. Ted also kept all the local bicycles on the road and always had a stock of broken bicycles hidden behind the stables and garage near to the lodge house which he used for spare parts. Mrs Dean, meanwhile, had many talents including selling cigarettes and tobacco, and taking in washing. She also made a nightly excursion to the kitchens at Meadowlands, never using the main drive from the lodge but rather a well-trodden path along the adjoining field hedge. The purpose of this was to collect the leftovers from the Dunkerley's meals – the family at the big house never ate cold meat – which she would then feed to her own family. The Deans' prudent lifestyle allowed them to help with the education of their three children and later the Dean offspring all had successful careers.

The Tunstalls and their Post Office

The post office near to Yew Tree farm was kept by the Tunstall family. The Tunstalls had a little garden and a very small farm where they kept one or two cows so that they could have their own milk and butter. When I knew them, Miss Ethel Tunstall came every morning to our farm for a jug of milk. Although our farms were on the same layer of gravel, our well water

The lodge at Meadowlands where Ted Dean, the 'Oogly Googly' man lived.

never tasted very nice, so Miss Tunstall came with her jug full of water and took our milk back in exchange. Mr Tunstall lived into his mid-nineties and continued with his job of collecting local rates and taxes right up to his death. His eventual demise was probably hastened by the fact that he once got knocked over and was badly injured crossing the treacherous A50 road.

A Whistle for a Telegram

In the 1930s and 1940s not many people had telephones and any urgent messages were received at local post offices and delivered as a telegram. One of the excitements for me as a young boy was when a telegram arrived at Tunstall's post office. At this point, Mrs Tunstall would blow a whistle. Upon hearing this, Mrs Dean, who would have the back door of the lodge house open while she worked through the day's washing, would leap onto her bicycle to pick the telegram up and then deliver it to its intended recipient.

In those days poorer ladies were not immaculately coiffeured. Most, like Mrs Dean, had the traditional bun held in place by hairpins, and a bonnet securely fastened by a large hatpin. Mrs Dean's bicycle had cords protecting the rear wheel to stop her skirts getting caught up in the spokes. At that time there was a film and stage act called 'Old Mother Riley.' Mrs Dean on her bicycle with bonnet and billowing skirt could have played the main character.

Charlie Stead – The Swearer

Charlie Stead was a builder who had been in the First World War and had only one eye. I got to know Charlie when he came to erect some wooden loose boxes for Father. He was on a fixed price so I knew that a bit of cheap labour would help and I set about assisting him.

Home of the Tunstall family.

I remember planing tongue-and-groove boards and nailing them on whilst we listened to Tommy Handley's programme on the wireless. Charlie revelled in this. In fact, he was one of the characters who introduced me to country humour and could always be relied upon for an apt phrase whatever the situation. He was once working on a bay window for the Dunkerleys, leaning out whilst planing the opening so it would fit better. Mrs Dunkerley's sister came into the room and exclaimed: 'Oh Stead, be careful!' He replied: 'Yes Ma'am, or it will be all slow walking and currant bread.' He was referring to the Cheshire custom of eating currant bread at a funeral.

Charlie's language wasn't very choice. He never used bad language in front of his wife, but I suppose he thought that, as a young farmer's boy, I needed educating and he certainly wasn't as careful in front of me. I used to ask him if he had shot many Germans in the war. His answer was always the same: 'Hundreds of the b★ggers'. I learned afterwards that he was in the Engineers and probably never even had a rifle!

TWO

Childhood at Yew Tree Farm

Milking, harvesting and dealing with the horses: that was life at Yew Tree Farm in the 1930s and 1940s. As I was the only son, Father needed to take on help with all the various activities and it's hardly surprising, therefore, that the main characters in my life as a young boy were those who worked on the farm or who lived and worked nearby.

Milking

In 1934, we started to sell milk from the farm. We had a herd of sixteen short horns and soon realised that we would need help with the milking. When I was nearly five, a new man came to work for Father as a milker. His name was Willy Moore and he replaced a chap called Joe Percival who had worked for the Wright family for many years. Joe was deaf and didn't communicate very well with my sister Joyce and me. Willy, on the other hand, was a talker. In fact he did his best to impress us with wonderful stories about his earlier life. We thought the world of him and he became one of the most important people in our childhoods. In the end, he was with our family for twenty-seven years.

Father employed Willy because of his experience with cattle: he was a very good milker. Willy came originally from a farm at Darnall, near Winsford and talked about his sister and brother who had their own farms. I don't know why he came to us as a worker, but he was always cheerful and showed no bitterness. At first, he lived in a flat in the local town of Knutsford, and would cycle to and from the farm. There were no weekends off or holidays for Willy because the cows had to be milked twice a day. We tried to finish early on a Saturday but Willy still came twice a day on a Sunday. In the winters of 1940 and 1942, we had had very heavy falls of snow and it must have been a struggle for him to get to us. Because of this, he must have decided at this point that it was time to move and he came to live in a house about a quarter of a mile away from the farm.

As a young child, I would often go down to the shippon at milking time. It was a lovely place, warm from the cows' hot breath and body heat. In fact, on a cold winter's morning, it was probably warmer than the farmhouse. Willy would sometimes encourage me to milk one of the teats of the cow he was milking. One night Father had a cow calving and Willy was helping him. There was no one to milk the cows. I reckoned I had to start sometime, and it seemed that this was my opportunity. No one was watching, so I thought to myself that it wouldn't matter if I made a mess of it and spilled some of the milk. I was much more successful than I thought I would be and when Willy and Father came back I had finished milking my first cow! They were rather surprised, but after inspecting the cow and the amount of milk, they pronounced that the cow was indeed milked. I was still at primary school at the time so I would have been about ten years old. Once you start something like that on a family farm you are not expected to stop. I was given the easy cows to milk at first.

Farm children on the farm cart, High Legh, 1930s.

But within a month or so my hands had got used to the work, and by the time I moved to secondary school, I was milking morning and night.

Milking was not something that everyone could do. It took skill and practice. It must have been sometime while I was still at school that the Agricultural Wages Board was set up and farm workers were granted one week of statutory holiday. For the first time ever, Willy had some time off and he and his wife went away to see their relatives. Despite my recently acquired talents in the milking department, Father thought we could do with some adult help so he approached George Bason, the gardener at Meadowlands. George had sometimes helped us at harvest time, and had clipped the garden and roadside hedges on Saturday afternoon. He was a typical country man: reliable, honest, and hard working. Mr Dunkerley had had Meadowlands professionally landscaped when it was built and with George's expertise it was soon one of the best gardens in the district. Superb gardener George might have been, but he was not a natural milker. He had milked cows in the past, but on this occasion – when we were employing him just for this task – he wasn't a great success. In fact, it took his hands the whole of the week to acclimatise to the job.

Prong in a Hay Stack

George Bason was a very even-tempered fellow. The only time Mother saw him upset was when she accidentally prodded him with the pikel while passing him sheaves on the stack at harvest time. Stacking sheaves was a skilled job, as the stacks had to be kept square with the sides either vertical or with a slight overhang. In the Dutch barns this was easier than it would have been outside as the stacker had the corner post for a guide. Some stackers used a pikel and most stood up to do the job, but George always knelt down. It doesn't need much imagination to realise where Mother had prodded him!

Threshing

I was always fascinated by threshing machines, so much so that when I was very young I pretended to have a threshing machine set of my own. My childhood pram, which was still around, was the engine, a grandfather chair became the threshing box and a small chair, the baler. I tied them together with string and pulled them round the house on the tiled floor. The whole contraption made a screeching noise that drove Mother wild.

The real threshing at Yew Tree Farm was done by George Bason's brother Billy who was a threshing machine driver with Barlows of High Legh. His traction engine was a Foster called Winnie. During the daytime, we children had to keep away from the machine, but after the threshing stopped for the night, we were allowed to go down to the stackyard. It was safe then; the belt had been taken off the thresher and everything was quiet. Winnie would be slumbering, and her boiler gurgling. The mice would be squeaking because their habitat had been disturbed and the cats would all be poised around the unthreshed stack waiting for their supper. The barn owl that could usually be seen at dusk wouldn't be about because of all the disruption.

A lot of preparation was needed before the threshing could start again next day. Winnie had a big thirst and, before we had mains water and a hose pipe, we had to provide tubs of water so that Billy Bason could quench her with bucketful after bucketful. Winnie also had a big appetite for coal. This, I was told, came from a seam under Manchester called 'Trench a Bone' and we used to go and pick it up at Heatley station, near Lymm. Winnie always seemed to relish her new supplies. Billy looked after her with loving care, feeding, watering and polishing her, often with an oilcan in his hand. He reckoned that after a day's threshing he – like Winnie – needed proper refreshment and, in his case, this meant a pint to wash down the dust. Unfortunately his wife didn't agree with him and she would often be waiting on the corner to intercept him on his way home. Billy soon grew wise to this and would choose his route home from Yew Tree Farm wisely!

Not my mother, but a typical Cheshire farmer's wife, High Legh, 1930s.

Winnie the traction engine outside the Kilton Inn. Her driver, Billy Bason, may have gone inside for a pint! Photographed by Lieutenant Ted Wurm who was stationed nearby with the US Army Air Corps, 1943.

Winnie's Revenge

Billy Bason went threshing in all the local parishes and, among other places, visited Hobbs Hill Farm, the home of my Auntie Gerty and Uncle Peter Cook (my father's sister and her husband). Their daughter, my cousin Gill, was a real bright spark who was always up to something and who frequently played tricks on people, including Billy. One morning, Billy had got Winnie, complete with her threshing box and baler, lined up on the road outside a local dairy farm called Halliwell's Brow. Cousin Gill came riding past on her bicycle, on her way to school. Just as she drew level with Winnie, she was engulfed in smoke and steam along with soot and dirty oil. When she got to school, Mr Cragg, the schoolmaster, had to take her into the schoolhouse to get her cleaned up. Billy Bason never accepted that he was responsible for Winnie's eruption just at that moment, but we all wondered.

I looked forward to growing up and using the threshing machine. As I grew older, I was allowed to go round it while it was working. Winnie was eventually replaced with a new engine called: 'King George V' which was operated by a chap called George Barlow. George had a hosepipe to keep the engine filled with water so that he was able to work the baler at the same time. There's a country song called 'The Old Threshing Mill' which always reminds me of just how the scene was in those days:

All over the valley you could hear the strange sound
Of that mighty machine on its annual round.
All the men in the town lands would follow at will
And they'd all lend a hand with the old threshing mill.

King George V is still seen at steam rallies.

The men who came round to the Cheshire farms with the threshing machines were a special breed. Some would carry bales on their backs and they seemed to delight in finding the longest ladders available so they could stack the bales right up to the roof of the sheds. The man cutting the strings on the sheaves controlled the scene. He was on top of the box, so he could see everything: the bale carriers skipping about, the man with the sack truck wheeling the bags of grain away and the man supplying him with the sheaves. One such man was a little guy called Harry Leigh. The only part of him that moved was the one arm with the knife on the end. He pulled the sheaves onto the other arm with his fingers, letting the released sheaf slide down into the machine. Apart from the arm, he was motionless for hours on end. He had nobody to talk to. Even when they stopped for 'baggin', Harry never spoke to anybody. A friend of mine reckoned he had been dead for ten years and nobody knew!

As we neared the end of the threshing, rats would start to run out of the stacks or bays of sheaves. As the Threshing Mill song goes, 'Along with the dogs and the cats/ We had the time of our life chasing after the rats.' The farm cats skulked around all through the threshing process as mice were to be found at any height among the sheaves. Rats, on the other hand, seemed to make their way just to the bottom layers. Rats were also often to be found under the old potato baskets against which we would rest the first sheaves of the harvest. To catch these, we would put some wire netting round the area being threshed to stop them getting away. A good dog was a great asset at this point and, in addition, we all had sticks. The workers pitching the sheaves would be killing the rats in between passing the sheaves on to the threshing machine. Father always reckoned that the best thing for killing rats was a muck fork with five prongs. With that, you could sometimes get five of them at once. Threshing was a dusty, hard job needing a minimum of seven workers. It was customary for Mother and Father to feed some of the regular machine workers, and friends or relations who had been asked to help. As the song said, 'Eight empty bellies would soon need a fill. It makes a man hungry does the old threshing mill.'

Those were the days: having baggin' during the haymaking season at Bingo Farm, *c.* 1939. From left to right: Uncle Frank, friend Alan Berry and Uncle Charlie. The dog is Jack, a specialist rat-catcher. This photograph appeared in the *Daily Herald*.

The Shippon

When I wasn't helping on the farm, I used to play in and around it with my playmate, Frank Brett. In the summer months we looked forward to Lewis's ice-cream van coming from Warrington. When we pestered mother for money, we could get ha'penny and penny cornets, and a special treat was a 'North Polar' (which was coated in chocolate). At odd times a man came along on a 'Stop-Me-And-Buy-One' three-wheeled cycle. He sold a frozen drink called 'Eldorado' in a paper wrapping. The trouble was you never knew when he was coming and we rarely had any money ready.

Frank and I had a favourite den in a shippon in the field next to the farm which was known as 'Tunstall's field. .We were not the only people to frequent this delightful building. It was also used as a 'mess room' by the local 'roadman,' Sam Blake, who kept his handcart under it. Sam's remit or 'length' covered the A50 road and the parishes of Mere and High Legh. 'Length men' like Sam did a good job keeping the road neat and tidy. Every Monday morning, Sam covered the whole length, picking up the litter that trippers had thrown out of their charabancs as they made their way to the Lancashire seaside resorts.

He had been a farm man, but there were benefits in working for the council including slightly lighter work and probably a pension on retirement. Sam swept the road, mowed the grass and cleaned the grids out on a regular basis. I don't think I ever saw a seedhead on a weed in that area.

Sometimes, in a very busy period, Sam had a helper called Harry Daniels who was affectionately known as 'Chummie' and who seemed to move around the area helping out. We always knew when these two were about to arrive. Chummie frequently whistled the signature tune of a music-hall act called Albert Whelan. Sam Blake wore corduroy trousers,

The old oak tree on Knutsford Road, High Legh, 1930s.

which swished as he walked along. So, we used to hear a melodious noise coming along the road, Sam's corduroys, Chummie's whistling and the axle on the handcart that needing oiling.

In the shippon, Sam Blake and Chummie chewed tobacco and threw their tea leaves on the floor. Spitting also seemed to be an accepted practice in there. As a result, the shippon had a horrible smell and Frank Brett and I used to have a competition as to who could stop in there the longest!

The Overcrowded Cottage

Sam Blake and his wife lived in a tiny two-up two-down cottage with a large number of children. My friend Ted Whittaker had a theory about how all the Blake children managed to sleep in that small dwelling place. He said that the youngest went to bed first and when he fell asleep, he was taken out and propped against the wall, thus vacating the bed for the next child! According to Ted, the process then continued until all the family had been catered for!

The Smithies

In the 1930s and 1940s, the best place to get news about the local area was at the blacksmiths. Sam Blake, the roadman, was a very good source of information because there were two smithies on his route along the A50. Gossip was exchanged between the blacksmiths and the farmers who brought their horses in to be shod on wet days. Sam would pass on whatever he heard to all those he encountered during the course of his work.

Shire horses remained the lifeblood of the farm.

The smithy at Mere went under the name of William Harkness. It was originally run by very enterprising blacksmiths who had made drill ploughs which were famous. In the 1930s and 1940s the Brett Brothers ran this business. James did the bookwork and sent out rather hefty bills. He made a lot of spelling mistakes but was, surprisingly, good with the figures! In my childhood, the Bretts still had a wheelwright's business making farm carts. On one occasion, Father took the balance plough to Bretts for repair. The blacksmith there was Arthur Ollier. He was nicknamed 'Oor' as making that noise was a mannerism of his. As we were loading the plough up that day, Father pointed out a new nut on the depth wheel. He explained to Arthur that the spanner supplied with the plough wouldn't fit it, so Arthur said 'Oor' and went off with the spanner, saying, 'I'll soon fix that.' He took the spanner to the fire with the intention of closing it up so it would fit the nut. Father pointed out that if he did that the spanner would then no longer fit the other nuts on the plough. Arthur just said 'Oor' and replaced the nut!

Renshaws at Primrose Hill was a smaller smithy business run by a father and son both called Arthur. The father was semi-retired when I knew him. Young Arthur was very good with me and Father often used to send me there with a horse to be shod. At that time, we had a young gelding called David; he had a nice temperament and was a good worker. What he loved best was being turned out into the field in the spring when he would gallop around the field kicking his heels into the air. Unfortunately, every time he did this he broke wind. It was very embarrassing, as he could be heard over a large area!

One day I was delegated to take David to the Renshaws. I had been before with our other horse, Dick, in the cart. As there was nothing to take or bring back this time, there was no cart and I, therefore, had the choice of walking alongside David or riding him. Father placed a large hessian sack on David's back with a rope to hold it in place. I decided to ride and held on to the rope, which was the only piece of tackle I had. David set off at a brisk trot. He was not as tall as a conventional shire but he was fat and had a large girth, so my little legs were spread very wide. It was about three miles to the smithy, and when I got there I was feeling the effect of the journey. The younger Arthur Renshaw took David's old shoes off while his father found new shoes to fit, worked the bellows on the fire and got the shoes ready for their first fitting.

The Farmer Who Never Stopped Talking

Blacksmiths were always busiest on the days when it was too wet for men to work on the farms. Then, farmers would come in to the smithies and talk. Whilst I was at Renshaw's smithy one day, a farmer called Harry Percival came in and started to chat. He arrived at the smithy at about 11.30 a.m. One of the blacksmiths went home for dinner at noon and got back about 2.00 p.m. to find Harry still talking! Harry was well known for his talkative ways. On another occasion, he went to Old Farm to see Uncle Frank. It was getting near bedtime, and in an effort to get Harry to leave, Auntie Bertha started to do all the bedtime chores: putting the cat out, winding up all the clocks and such like. But Harry apparently completely ignored all these signals and just carried right on talking.

Once the job was finished, I was helped back on board David and we set off at a brisker trot than before, even though he had heavier shoes to pick up. Just like his predecessor, Blossom, and all other horses, David always went faster on the way home. The journey back was far worse than the one there. In a narrow part of the road we met a large transport vehicle – a Scammel Articulated – which was chain-driven. The chains used to wear and lengthen so they made a loud flapping noise. Although he had a quiet temperament, even David couldn't put up with this. He increased speed. The din got worse after we'd passed the vehicle, and David went faster still. I was thrown about all over the place. It was the last time I went to the smithy astride a horse.

Daisy the Goat

Perhaps because we lived on a farm, I only ever had one animal that you could call a pet. Daisy was a goat who sometimes used to terrify people. I had her for many years and eventually she had kids of her own and I milked her. In the early days, however, she was useful for keeping the grass low at nearby Swiss Cottage. This had a large garden which had been grassed over at some point. Father had looked after it originally, cutting the grass himself and making it into hay. When I got the goat, however, this was one fewer job for Father to do. I used to tether Daisy out every day in the grass-growing season.

Goats are real characters; they have no fear and they will charge at anything. Daisy would sharpen up her horns on the wall of the old pigsty where she was kept. If somebody came to visit, I would let her loose and she would run along the low wall round the midden area which was topped with rounded coping stones. She was very agile and could jump over all sorts of obstacles, much to the delight of those watching. My cousin Winnie came one evening and was teasing Daisy by taking hold of her horns so that she couldn't move. When she let go, Daisy went for a gallop round the yard and sneaked up behind Winnie before headbutting her and knocking her right over!

High Legh School

Going to school seemed nothing more than a bit of a distraction after everything that was happening on the farm. From 1936, I attended High Legh School, a small Church of England establishment with three classes and three teachers. The windows in the school were high

My pet goat Daisy and me, *c.* 1942. I am wearing the uniform of Lymm Grammar School.

up and you couldn't see out of them. When one of the teachers was absent, Mrs Cragg, the headmaster's wife, used to step in. She had been a teacher in her younger days and she was quite strict. If you were even a little bit naughty, Mrs Cragg made you stand on the form as a punishment. The good thing about this was that you could see the traffic going past. It meant that if I was naughty at school, at least I could tell Father whose horses had gone to the smithy that day! I remember one day, more than half the boys in the class were made to stand on the form. Mr Cragg soon sorted them out. He was a good schoolteacher and also ran a football team in his younger days. He was very well respected, perhaps because he had two leather straps for punishment. The one with three tails was for very severe punishment. One of my classmates reckoned that although we could all stand a good telling off from Mrs Cragg, we couldn't stand the strap. After Mr Cragg had finished with you, you didn't want to stand on the form. You didn't want to sit on it either.

Mr Cragg and Mrs James, the infant teacher, and the rest of the staff, had high educational standards and many children from High Legh passed scholarships and went onto grammar schools. If you weren't very attentive Mr Cragg had his own method of getting your attention. He was a sure shot with a piece of chalk. One afternoon, a boy was sitting 'gawping' with his mouth wide open — suddenly he was brought back to reality as a piece of chalk landed in his mouth.

Free School Milk

In 1943, whilst I was still at High Legh School, free school milk was introduced. We were supposed to drink this in the morning break. It was pasteurised, so it wasn't quite what we farm children were used to drinking at home. I suppose, however, it was safer for us. We didn't like the taste at all and I know before the milk came along we used to look forward to the warm summer months when we could just have water. The milk did come in useful on occasions though. When Mrs Cragg made us cocoa with water and no sugar at lunchtime, we were glad to slip in a little milk — pasteurised or not.

High Legh School, built in the 1890s on the site of another school. The building was used as a school until the 1960s, and is now High Legh Village Hall.

Tatton Hall, the south front view from the grounds.

A local band stops the traffic in High Legh, 1930s.

Cheshire hounds at High Legh Hall, one of several important stately homes in the neighbourhood.

The Local Country Estates

In the 1930s and 1940s, the character of the local countryside was still determined by the gentry who controlled the country estates. Whilst I was at school, you had to touch your forelock when you met the local squire at the High Legh Sports Day held at nearby High Legh Hall. We once had a wonderful school trip out – the result of an official invitation – to another local stately home, Tatton Park, the home of Lord Egerton. I think we had tea that day in the Tenants' Hall. I didn't see that room again for many years but when I did, I remembered very distinctly the animal heads on the wall and the impression they had made on me as a boy.

That day, at Tatton, we were under the supervision of our teachers but the vast expanse of the Park soon proved too much for them and they couldn't control us. We started running off in all directions. I'm sorry to say that any child who was unable to keep up with those of us at the front was left behind. We were about to be taught a lesson, however. Later on in the day, we were amazed to see one of the poor souls that we had abandoned riding around with his Lordship in his motor – a Benz Comfort Car – registered 'M1.' As with so many things, this was a lesson in life that just couldn't be learned in the schoolroom.

THREE

The War Years

In 1939, the impending war was something that everybody feared. I suppose the memories of the First World War were in most people's minds and all the locals mourned the large number of soldiers who had never returned. Our neighbours, the Tunstalls, had lost their sons Willie and Frank within just a month of each other. People thought that the First World War had been the war to end all wars and couldn't believe that they had to face another. My friend Harry Jones was very despondent about the prospect of another war and thought that we should all jump into the Dam at Lymm to escape whatever was coming. It's a good job that nobody followed his advice because Lymm Dam was the local source of drinking water.

The lives of many of the local farmers and farm workers were totally changed by the Second World War. As well as continuing to run Old Farm, Uncle Frank became an air raid warden. This was probably better for him than the Home Guard would have been because, after his experiences in the First World War, he had said that if was given a rifle, he would shoot the first German he saw. For his new role, Uncle Frank was issued with a greatcoat, which was a heavy overcoat to keep you warm on winter nights when out during air raids. Uncle Frank welcomed the coat with relish as he reckoned it would make a good rug for the 'tits' when he had finished with it. The 'tit' was a local, affectionate name given to a horse. In winter, after being in a warm stable, horses were covered with rugs to keep them warm outside before the effort of work warmed them up.

Willie Moore, our milking man, joined the Home Guard. He was tall and slim and used to shake a little. It was something that never got worse, but it must have caused some concern when he was issued with a rifle. Everything around him was at more risk than the target he was aiming at! Some way into the war, the Home Guard was issued with Sten guns. We liked to think that these were more appropriate for Willie as the automatic fire meant that there was a much better chance of him hitting something!

The Army at High Legh Hall

The war also brought many changes to the local area. High Legh Hall and surrounding buildings were used as an Army camp and this brought in many workers from other areas. Mrs Atkinson (our neighbour who lived in Swiss Cottage), had four lodgers who worked at the camp at one time. Despite the fact there was only one large and one small bedroom in the cottage, no bathroom and an outside pan toilet, Mrs Atkinson seemed to cope all right. One of the lodgers, George James, recalled that the men had weekend ablutions out on the yard and that Mrs Atkinson worked the pump. She reckoned she had seen it all before so she wasn't bothered!

Entrance to High Legh Hall, where the Army was based.

The Resourceful Widow

Mrs Atkinson had already been a widow once and Mr Atkinson was her second husband. She was a resourceful woman. At her second wedding at Rostherne Church, the best man fumbled with the wedding ring at the altar steps and it fell through a metal grid in the floor which led to the heating pipes. Without any panic, Mrs Atkinson slipped off her wedding ring from her previous marriage and suggested that the vicar use that. It may not have been very romantic, but at least there was no hold up in the ceremony!

The Army camp at High Legh consisted of a lot of huts and new buildings – garages, workshops and a NAAFI. The West Hall, which was part of the complex, was the officers' mess. I believe concerts were held in the NAAFI to which local people were invited. There were also lawns and a grass tennis court which had become overgrown. Father was contracted to cut them and Willie Moore and I helped him. We went up there on our bicycles, Willie with a scythe, and I with a sickle. When we arrived, we were greeted by an officer with a large moustache and a drink in his hand who enquired what we were doing. When we told him he said: 'Good show, jolly good show.' On being told that Father was on the way with the horses and mowing machine he said: 'Prang wizard.' I had heard this sort of talk on the radio but I had never thought that people might speak like that in real life.

We were lucky in that during some of the harsh winters of the 1940s, the soldiers at the camp were on hand to dig a road through the snow on the A50. They also kept clear many of the small country lanes that had filled with snow blown off the adjoining fields. The regiment at High Legh was mainly the South Lancashire, but, at one time, there were the ATS ladies as well. I remember the son of one of the ATS staying with us and sharing my bedroom for a short while. He was on holiday from school. This was a bit of a surprise to me but I agreed after Mother explained it was something we could do to help the war effort.

Above and below: Thank goodness for the Army: soldiers from the nearby Army camp set about clearing the snow in the very cold winter of 1942.

Father had rented part of High Legh Park before the war and it was still let to him. We used to take our cows across the A50 road to this piece of land on a regular basis. As this was grassland and couldn't be ploughed up, it was suggested that the Army might use it for training. They would line their motors up along the A50 road before entering the field and we knew they were there because smoke bombs would sometimes go off among the cows. Quite surprisingly none of the animals was ever hit. Sometimes, however, the bombs fell into Wrenshot Cottage garden, just across the road from our farm. If this happened, the incident would immediately be followed up by a visit from an officer to apologise.

At the beginning of the war, the perimeter of a prisoner of war camp was erected near to Yew Tree Farm with a drive onto the A50 road. It was quite secure with a fence made from three rolls of barbed wire. We were told that the camp would be very useful for imprisoning the Germans if we were ever invaded. We always wondered, of course, whether the Germans would end up putting us in the camp if the invasion was successful. The grass inside the camp enclosure looked lush and inviting – just the sort of pasture our cows would enjoy. In order not to waste it, Father cut a hole in the fence to allow the cows access. He made the hole near to a pond with trees round it, so that it wouldn't be noticed. Presumably, the prisoners themselves never found out about it!

Several prisoners of war came to work at High Legh. They were of all nationalities, although mainly Germans and Italians. The Germans had a pride in themselves: they were going to show the English how good they were and they very soon adapted to any job or task they were asked to do. Two Germans also worked for my cousin at Broad Heyes Farm, further down the A50 at the west end of High Legh. Willie had come from a farm in Westphalia and drove a team of horses, Heinz did general work; if they were working together Heinz took the heavier tasks.

At Yew Tree Farm, we had only one prisoner of war, a German named George. He too was a very good worker. All of the Germans insisted that Germany was a good country to live in, and that it was very prosperous under the rule of Hitler. The good thing about them as far as we were concerned was that they seemed to accept authority without complaint. I often wondered how the British Tommy was faring working on German farms. Had he the same enthusiasm? The Italian prisoners of war were different from the Germans and worked as little as possible. We also had some prisoners of other nationalities – men who had joined up with the German Army from allied countries and were, therefore, collaborators. These prisoners were kept separate from the Germans and Italians. They were French, Moroccan, and South Tyrolian and seemed to have no enthusiasm for work at all. And we had a Yugoslavian who had been in the Luftwaffe. He was a nice young man who told us that when his country had been overrun he had volunteered. He admitted it was a mistake and I think he had been glad to be captured.

The US Airforce

Perhaps the people causing the most concern on the A50 road during the war years were the American forces who in 1944 started driving past to the US airforce base at Burtonwood, Warrington. When the British Army drove past, they went in convoy at slow speed with a red flag at the front and a green at the rear. The RAF or Ministry of Supply would carry parts of planes past on vehicles called 'Queen Marys' which were large but didn't cause any concern. The Americans, however, caused a lot of trouble because of the speed at which they drove. Sometimes they were going so fast, they couldn't pull up in time. They travelled in convoy: the trucks were driven by black drivers with a white officer in charge. The officer travelled at the back in a jeep and was on hand to sort out any problems.

Yew Tree Farm is on an 'S' bend – which means that it was and still is a high spot for accidents. The six-wheeled Diamond T and Mack All-Wheel drive trucks couldn't negotiate the bend at all. One day Father and I were taking the cows across the road as usual when they ran foul of an American convoy. This was the only time we had a cow killed and one injured. On another occasion, the driver braked on the bend and skidded sideways up the road until the rear wheels hit the kerb. When the vehicle jolted, the driver must have taken his foot off the brake. It was still in gear so it went straight forward into the field where I was pulling up mangolds with Willie. We heard the screech of brakes and Willie shouted, 'Run!' The truck slithered to a stop right where I had been working. A large black man descended from the truck and surveyed the scene. He looked at the mangolds and said, 'I reckon these are about ready for picking.' Then he got back in his truck, and reversed out of the field in a shower of soil and mangold foliage!

This type of incident with the American drivers happened quite often. One truck narrowly missed a council workmen's hut on the grass verge, complete with occupants, and instead demolished the handcart which stood alongside. I must say, there was never any trouble regarding compensation for damage from the Americans, provided they had an officer with them. They went into the field so often I think they regarded it as part of the highway. Often though, it was a lone truck, there was no damage to the vehicle, and they were gone before you could get any details.

War in the Sky

From just before the war, aeroplanes were becoming more popular. We were always thrilled when a plane came into Manchester (then called Ringway) Airport. Some of the early aeroplanes must have been the forerunners of KLM and we would refer to them as Flying Dutchmen. There was also a small red bi-plane which often came in from Barton Aerodrome.

The Facts of Life

As a boy, I could never understand where all our new calves came from. Willie Moore reckoned that they were brought in on the small red bi-plane that we sometimes saw overhead. I believed this for a while, until I started to discuss the matter with other children at school and until I saw what the bull was doing!

During the war, we used to be able to see the parachutists practising at Tatton Park, sometimes jumping out of a balloon and basket, sometimes out of a troop-carrying plane. Sometimes, the sky seemed to be full of parachutes. Other aircraft that came into the country – The Luftwaffe - were, of course, not so welcome. Out in Cheshire, we didn't get the incessant bombing in the way that the big cities did. The bombs that fell near us were probably dropped by German bombers which had lost their way to or from Manchester. Mostly we just had scary moments, but there were two tragedies. One of these was caused by a bomb hitting one of the back lodges at Dunham Massey Hall near Altrincham. When we drove past the scene a few days later, we were shocked to see the lodge completely obliterated with clothes hanging from the trees. The other tragedy took place at Over Alderley on 3 December 1940. On this occasion, four children were left without a mother or father. Quite a few other bombs exploded in the area. One was very near to the West Hall at High Legh – the officers' mess. I suspect they had some suitable adjectives to describe the incident. In fact, they were quite lucky, as a large tree took most of the impact.

At Yew Tree Farm, we had an air-raid shelter in what was then the orchard. This was shared with our neighbours Jack and Dorcas Heesom. They had come to live in Legh Cottage after the Tunstalls left. Jack was a bricklayer on the High Legh Estate – a good tradesman with a dry sense of humour – who had helped to dig the shelter out. I remember going in the shelter on only one occasion. On the other nights we hid under the kitchen table. The worst local bombing was a breadbasket of incendiary bombs that fell on the farm next to ours – Goodiers Green Farm. I remember that the whole area was lit up with hedges ablaze. The loft over the shippon was hit and set alight. It most probably had hay in it. Luckily, the Shore family who lived there were out visiting relatives that evening. Strangely, as if he had had a premonition of what was about to happen, Mr Shore had felt uneasy that evening, so they came home early. Fortunately this meant that the family were on hand to untie the chains and get the cows out of the shippon away from the flames. The Shore's son, Douglas, who was a very young boy, helped his father. Muriel, their daughter, went further down the road to some other neighbours, the Hewitts, and stayed under the stairs.

Blackout at the Farm

During the war, all windows at the farm had to be blacked out. The police and air raid wardens were very keen that no lights at all were showing. Willie even went to the trouble of screwing a little swivel piece of plywood over the finger holes on the farm building doors. At the opposite extreme, there was a large beacon that was towed to different sites in the area with the deliberate intention of lighting the place up. We presumed this was to attract the German bombers to less populated areas. One night this beacon was stationed in one of our fields. Father went to tell those in charge that he didn't think it was a very good idea. He was firmly told it was no business of his, or words to that effect.

Food Production

The war made a big difference to local life. For local farmers, it was not like the First World War, because fewer of them joined the forces. This time round, the main priority was food production. Women were affected as much as men; most farmers' daughters worked at home on the farm in some capacity, perhaps looking after the laying hens, or, in some areas, producing cheese. The Land Army was the start of many other girls from the towns coming to help on the farms. It was a complete change of lifestyle for them but they were very enthusiastic and soon became a vital part of the labour force. In our area there were two hostels for the girls; others lived on the farms where they worked. Many of the girls from the Land Army got married to local boys and some still live in the area today. Some of them married farmers' sons and ended up as farmers' wives.

Any Life Boy?

There was a story told about one Land Army girl who went to live with an old bachelor farmer. After the day's work she wanted a bath, so she was instructed where the tin bath was kept. She decided to take it upstairs, followed by the water which she had to heat up. On undressing she realised she had no soap so she duly went down the stairs to the farmer to enquire whether he had any 'Lifebuoy!' The old man nearly died of shock.

With the war came the rationing of food. One of the perks of farming was that you were allowed to keep a pig for your own use. We used to work out a rota with the other local

Sheila Browne (later Norbury) came from
Ireland to be a Land Girl in Cheshire, 1948.

farms so that we killed our animals at different times and then shared the meat. The pig was
fed all the scraps such as potato peelings together with some of the corn that we were using
to feed the hens and the milking cows. All feedstuffs were rationed and we got coupons for
more from the Ministry of Agriculture based on the amount of eggs and milk that we sold
from the farm. All the wheat we produced had to be sold, but we could keep some oats for
feeding to the stock we owned. Killing the pig was a great event. We didn't have our own
bench or turnell (a wooden bath like a shallow barrel) to scald it in, so we borrowed those.
At first, Uncle Peter Cook would come and kill the pig. Mother was entrusted with ensuring
that the water was near boiling point when he arrived. She was very concerned lest she
encountered his wrath and I remember that she made every effort to light the fire under the
boiler in plenty of time.

Humane killers (bolt action guns to stun the animal) were not compulsory at that time so it
was a big job keeping the pig on the bench. Uncle Peter was a good butcher and he sawed up
the carcass in such a way that there were no shattered bones. The pig would be about twenty
score in weight: that is 400lbs. The first bacon cured would be the cheeks, which tasted nice
and sweet, after being in salt for only about a week. We usually had half the pig and gave the
other half to our neighbours. They would do the same for us. In the case of a big pig, the pork
only came from the ribs so there was no fat or rind on it. The idea was to get as much bacon
as possible, as there were no fridges or freezers to keep the pork fresh. There would be about
an inch of fat on the bacon and ham. The bacon, to me, was lovely, particularly when the rind
was cooked crisp. One of the perks of the pig killing was that a football would be fashioned
from the pig's bladder for we children to play with.

In the early 1940s, the law changed and it became compulsory to use humane killers. We
dispensed with Uncle Peter Cook and had to find another butcher. The trouble was that this

one used a cleaver to cut up the carcass, and this meant that we got shattered bones in the meat. I remember Mother making brawn out of the pig's head and picking the bones out of it after it had been boiled. Uncle Frank once came up to the farm and saw her doing it. He was always finicky about food and he went home and told Auntie Bertha he wasn't having any of that 'jollop'. In the First World War, when he was in the trenches, he had had a lot of corned beef, which he called 'bully beef'. The brawn was very similar in appearance and Uncle Frank wasn't having any of it.

The Egg-loving Policeman

Keeping hens on the farm meant that, despite rationing, we always had a good supply of eggs. Our local policeman used to ride up on his bike on regular visits and invariably went back with some. There was an outbreak of Foot and Mouth disease during the war and there were rules and regulations about what you could and couldn't do with cattle. One day, we were taking our cows as usual across the A50 road when the egg-loving policeman rode up on his bike and booked us for an offence. Father had mistakenly been under the impression that (as the cows were only being moved to another part of our own farm), he didn't need a Movement Permit. The policeman fined Father and warned him about any further transgressions. Father wasn't very happy about this; local policemen usually dropped a hint before booking you, and Father said as much. Needless to say, the policeman never called again for his eggs.

School During The War

Life at school changed at the beginning of the war. Air-raid shelters were built in the schoolyard and sometimes we had exercises in which we had to evacuate the school. I only remember two occasions when we had a proper alarm at school because most of the air raids were at night. The biggest disruption at school came with the arrival of the evacuees from Manchester. For a number of weeks the school operated a shift system with the village children having lessons on one shift and the evacuees on the other. The evacuees' own teachers came with them. After a while, a lot of the evacuees went back to the city and the rest were integrated into the school with only one of their teachers remaining. This is when we got to know each other better, and more than a few fights ensued!

Several evacuees remained in the North Cheshire area until the end of the war, and some for many years afterwards. The ones I knew of stayed with families who had no children of their own. One boy, Tony Keenan, lived on a farm in High Legh for many years after the others had returned home. In later years, when I started going to dances, I met a girl who had been an evacuee and who had stayed with Mr Bert Shore – a traveller for a farmers' Co-op. Mr Shore was a jovial character, and I am sure that this girl must have had a good family life with the Shores. That's probably why she stayed so long. The funny thing is, I can't remember her name – we always referred to her simply as 'Bert's Evac'.

Much to the surprise of the area, in 1942 I passed a scholarship and went to Lymm Grammar school. I was not an academic. In my first history lesson we had to write down why we should take history as a subject, and unfortunately I couldn't think of anything to say. Our history teacher, Titch Harland, was very disappointed with my efforts. She enquired where I came from, and when I said I came from a farm, she told me that she had also come from a farm in her younger days. She said we could make a deal: if I behaved myself she wouldn't force me to learn history. At the time, our arrangement was fine, but in later years, my lack of academic effort came to be something I regretted.

The War and the Dunkerleys

During the war, the Dunkerley family were still the owners of Meadowlands. Mr Dunkerley had passed on, leaving Mrs Dunkerley on her own. The children whom Mother had looked after before her marriage still kept in touch. Arthur was married and living away. Donald had risen up the ranks and was the commander of a submarine in the navy; he sent Mother Christmas cards every year and once even included a book of poems he had written. Mary Dunkerley was the closest to my mother and she came for tea every Friday. She was my sister Joyce's godmother, and was invaluable to Mother, taking her to Pendlebury hospital to visit Joyce when my sister was admitted for a four-week period when she was four years old. Mary seemed quite glamorous to me. She had a sports car and was a very keen horsewoman who went hunting regularly. Apparently, she met her husband, John Marsh, on a hunt. Mary visited us on a regular basis after her marriage, and always on Christmas morning to drop off a present before they went to Meadowlands for Christmas Dinner.

The fourth Dunkerley child Eric (or 'Mr Eric' as he was known to me) had married his childhood sweetheart, Phyllis Langford-Brooke, from Mere Hall. They had a house built across the field down Wrenshot Lane. Wrenshot Cottage was a lovely place, thatched, with oak beams inside that had been taken from a building that had been demolished at Yew Tree Farm. Mr Eric was a senior partner in the business of C.C. Dunkerley Steel Stockholders in Store Street, Manchester. Like everything, Mr Eric's business was affected by the war. He used to go to France to purchase steel, but after Dunkirk that came to an end. Steel making was a reserved occupation and Mr Eric was, therefore, not eligible to be called up for the armed forces. Like everyone else, however, he wanted to be involved in the war effort. He decided that he could run the steel business on a part-time and 'wet day' basis – that is, he would work on the business if it was raining and on one of the Dunkerley's three farms if it was fine.

In time, Mr Eric bought a tractor and farm machinery, taking advice from a mechanically-minded young man in the locality named Jack Wright. The first tractor bought by Mr Eric was an Allis-Chalmers Model C with rollers, disc harrow and a trailer. This was how the mechanization of farming began for me. The binder, which had been one of the worst machines for horses to pull, was now converted so that it could be pulled by a tractor. The Allis-Chalmer was not as powerful as the standard Fordson that was becoming popular, but it was more advanced in some respects having lights and a self-starter. It also had a cushioned bench seat which could accommodate two people. It was 1943. I would only have been eleven but I was ready – and desperate – to drive a tractor.

Like his father, Mr Eric was a wonderful man to work with. It was not long before he bought a small Nicholson baler. I was part of the team who tied the wires and slid in the blocks to separate the bales. One day I became a bit casual and didn't slide the block in straight – it jammed the baler and threw the belt off. I was expecting my marching orders and I offered to go but I was simply told that I wasn't concentrating and that I should get on with the job. Mr Eric was also someone who helped me to appreciate rural humour. One day, a man came into the yard with a very large red nose: after he had gone, Mr Eric claimed it 'must have cost hundreds of pounds to develop a nose like that!'

Of the three farms owned by the Dunkerleys, Holly House Farm, let to Albert Percival (known as Albi), was the smallest. Albi didn't have any milking cows so he lent a hand on all three farms. He was a tall, strongly built man who had been in the artillery in the First World War, looking after the horses. He had a sweetheart who played the organ at Rostherne church, but it never seemed to come to anything. She looked after her mother and Albi's spinster sister Patty lived with him.

In those days, when we were harvesting, Albi was on the binder and Mr Eric drove the tractor. As we got to the last bit of corn to be cut, the rabbits in the corn would bolt. They would come out at full speed. Shooting at them, with workers all around setting up the sheaves in stooks, could be a dangerous pursuit. Albi Percival had developed his own personal way

I couldn't wait to drive the Allis Chalmers Model C. Here, I've just finished 'ridging up' for potatoes, 1947.

of catching rabbits. The corn would be sown in rows, and Albi would watch to see if there was a rabbit running down a row anywhere near to him. If there was, he would step down off the binder, straddling the correct row, and as the rabbit went between his legs, his hand would drop down to pick the animal up. After a quick twist of the wrist, Albi would be back on the binder.

The Dunkerley's suffered their own tragedy during the war. Donald Dunkerley (affectionately known as 'Dunk') was the lieutenant commander of H.H. submarine *Thames*. The submarine was lost in 1940 and there were no survivors. Donald had been married to a Mrs Lolly who had previously been married to his commanding officer. Somehow, she and Dunk had got together. As a widow, this lady came to stay at Meadowlands to be with her mother-in-law during their bereavement. That harvest time, the weather was good. It was not long before Mr Eric invited his sister-in-law to join the harvest team: she could, after all, sit on the other side of the tractor seat. The young Mrs Dunkerley appeared in the shortest pair of shorts ever seen in a harvest field. Perhaps I was too young to appreciate the situation but I remember Father telling Mother that the men had had a terrible day workwise. He reckoned that Willie Moore and Albi Percival were all of a lather over the young woman in her shorts!

During the war, old Mrs Dunkerley lived on her own at Meadowlands, apart from a maid, Maggie, and a cook called Annie Power. Willie Moore had met Maggie whilst delivering potatoes. She was known as the 'Merry Widow,' and Willie was obviously enamoured by her. He once turned up in his best clothes at the end of the Dunkerley's drive and it gave us all something to talk about. Annie Power was one of Mother's cronies. She would come across to see us at the farm before we went to bed and tell us all the gossip. She was like a music-hall act and I remember in particular that she told us stories about a niece of the Dunkerleys who had been staying at the big house, and who was a little eccentric. This girl had one day somehow managed set her bed on fire. Annie explained, with all the appropriate dramatic actions, how

"DUNKS"

TRIBUTE TO SUBMARINE COMMANDER

"A.H.D." has contributed to the "Times," the following tribute to the late Lieut.-Commander W. D. Dunkerley, R.N., of Mere, who commanded H.M. Submarine Thames, recently reported lost :—

The death of Lieut.-Commander W. D. Dunkerley, R.N., has robbed the Navy of an able submarine commander and his friends of a unique personality. "Dunks," as he was always known, had a love of words and phrases which was refreshing in a world where language has become so dull and sterotyped. He will be remembered by many for the pithy and provocative statements which at first alienated strangers, who expected a commonplace remark, but their interest was soon aroused, and they invariably came for more. He wrote, and though few saw any of his work there is no doubt that given time and patience he would have accomplished something enduring. He had a love of the land which went very deep, and nothing gave him greater pleasure than scything or cutting down a tree. He was different from us all, and we mourn him

PERSONAL TRIBUTE
LIEUTENANT-COMMANDER W. D. DUNKERLEY, R.N.

R. P. R. writes :—

I served with "Dunks" in more than one ship and for nearly three years, and the most striking side of his character was his extraordinary kindness and generosity. His apparently cynical utterances were never vindictive and hid a personality that felt other people's sufferings acutely. An argument with "Dunks"—which he loved—was always an entertainment. He was a wonderfully true friend, who would be more than surprised to know how many people miss him.

The disappearance of Donald Dunkerley made it into the *Times* in 1940.

she had bundled the mattress out of the window. Annie was also a great mimic and could 'take off' local characters such as George Bason and his brother-in-law, Harry Pickering. These two walked with what was locally known as 'the gait' as their joints were getting a bit the worse for wear. Annie would get up out of the chair, walking in their style with arms flailing, and give a running commentary. She was a scream and Joyce and I were always in hysterics listening to her.

Mother always respected Mrs Dunkerley and the affection was returned. The old lady would come across with her dog and take Joyce on nature tours, mainly down Dobb Lane. She also bought books on wild flowers for Joyce's Christmas presents. Mother and Joyce used to visit the garden at Meadowlands and very often I was allowed to fish the pond. Mother was sure it wasn't very deep. Many years later my son Andrew cleaned it out and I was amazed at the depth – probably about 15ft. Mrs Dunkerley tried to help with the war effort in various different ways. She was a Wartime National Savings Agent and bought Joyce and me our first saving certificates. In fact, she visited many local families and encouraged them to save. Sometimes when we had earned a bit of money or had been given money as a present, we went across to Meadowlands to entrust it to Mrs Dunkerley's safekeeping.

First Aid at Meadowlands

Mrs Dunkerley was involved with the WVS and organised local ladies in First-Aid activities. I once got involved as a volunteer patient. The instruction was in the playroom at Meadowlands. I was requested to enter the room and fall down the steps pretending to break my leg. Unfortunately, I ended up lying on the wrong side and I had to do it all over again as the WVS ladies had not practised tending to that leg!

Mrs Dunkerley was a regular churchgoer and used to drive to the church in Rostherne several times a week. Because it was wartime, petrol was rationed. On the application form for petrol coupons there were a series of questions including whether or not you had an alternative form of transport such as a bicycle. Being an honest and upright lady, Mrs Dunkerley had recorded on her form that she did have such alternatives, and of course, her petrol rations were duly curtailed. She came across to see Mother disappointed with the result and wanting some advice. Mother knew that although it was rationed, petrol was available for essential journeys like shopping and religious visits. After quite a bit of discussion Mother advised Mrs Dunkerley to apply again, to state her age and also to get a letter of support from the vicar of Rostherne. This she did and she was rewarded with more petrol coupons. She showed her delight by generously picking up local people on their way to church.

That was rural life during the war – everybody helped each other out.

FOUR

Local Life After the War

As the war ended, I left school. Probably I should have stayed on until I was sixteen, but Father wasn't too well and I wanted to leave, so the Education Authorities agreed that I could go at fourteen. There was an old saying that farmers' children only went to school on wet days and it is definitely true that I had already taken a lot of time off to help on the farm.

The mid-1940s was an interesting time to be working on a farm because it was the period just before mechanisation really took off. Father had bought the tractor and machinery from Mr Eric but we were still using the balance plough at times, pulling it with the tractor. It was all right as long as you had an oilcan at hand to keep the wheels lubricated. We were also still using a team of horses for ploughing in the wet winter months, sowing corn and working in the potatoes. My first year of proper work was a year of transition on the farm; I sometimes drove the horses, but I increasingly spent a lot of time on the tractor. I wasn't yet allowed to drive on the road, so my sister Joyce helped me out when we needed to move it down the A50.

The Changing Face of the A50

The A50 passing right outside Yew Tree Farm has been a source of continuing fascination for me. After the war, it saw big changes. The days of teams of horses taking goods into Manchester were over, as were the days of farmers taking milk by horse to the local station. With the new availability of road transport, some farmers' sons bought lorries and started carrying milk to dairies in the towns in the mornings. In the afternoon, they would unload the empty milk churns and use their lorries for other sorts of farm haulage work. Gradually, these piecemeal efforts turned into full-blown road-haulage businesses.

For farmers, road haulage was really just a continuation of what they had been doing with the horses – it was a fairly easy business transition for them to make. But what these small businesses were able to do depended very much on the category of road license they had. Having a Type A licence meant that you could carry anything anywhere. Type B restricted both the mileage you were allowed to do and the goods you were allowed to carry. Type C licences were for firms delivering their own goods or lorries that were on contract to the manufacturer. A lot of operators went broke because they had bought lorries on credit and were trying too hard to undercut each other's rates. The rules and regulations didn't help because they meant that a lot of lorries had to make return journeys empty – something which, obviously, brought profits down.

Before the building of the M6, the A50 road was one of the main west coast routes joining the Potteries with the A6 road to Scotland. Drivers found that the towns en route were too busy to negotiate during in the daytime, and so heavy traffic would run right through the night. Although the speed of vehicles was limited to 20mph, we still had accidents. Nearly

Sticking to the old methods: Uncle Frank and Yvonne turning the hay, late 1950s.

all of these were caused by northbound lorries and happened in the early morning, probably because the drivers had gone to sleep. On one occasion, a Liverpool-bound lorry smashed into the gates at Yew Tree Farm in the early hours and completely demolished them. Charlie Stead, the local builder and I replaced them and, in doing so, we widened the entrance to the farm to its present width.

I used to enjoy watching the lorries from all the different haulage firms going past. In my memory, they are all smartly painted and gleaming with chrome. They were all British built with different-sounding diesel engines. From long hours of listening to the traffic, even when I couldn't see the vehicle, I could distinguish what it was from the particular noise of its engine. Lorries with Gardner engines made the windows at Yew Tree Farm buzz as they went past and caused us some problems with loose panes.

Many different products travelled up and down the A50. To name but a few – we had linoleum coming past from Dundee, Massey Harris Farm machinery from Kilmarnock, and steel pipes from Coatbridge (also in Scotland). There were vehicles from Robson's haulage firm from Carlisle, Bowkers from Blackburn, and Suttons from St Helens, Preston, Liverpool, Wigan and Warrington. These vehicles were all going south, of course. Goods from Birmingham, Coventry and the Potteries, on the other hand, were all going north to the Liverpool Docks and the North of England.

And then suddenly after the war, all this changed. In 1947, the Labour government brought in the Transport Act. Overnight, road transport was nationalised and in the place of private haulage firms came British Road Services. Somehow, this change seemed to affect the whole character of the A50. Now all the lorries were the same colour and, although they had a regional area written on the side of them, you had no real idea where they came from or where they were going to. From my point of view, it was also disappointing that they all sounded the same as well. The families who had run haulage firms had to turn to other ways of making money. Many bought farms in the area. A Mr Allen from Stalybridge, for example, bought Bowdon View Farm, and a Mr Taylor bought a farm in High Legh. Both had previously been haulage firm owners.

A privately owned lorry before the nationalisation of British Road Services in 1947

Accounts

From the age of twelve I had taken on some of the administrative duties at the farm. With the increasing number of employees, somebody needed to be able to deal with the PAYE. Father hadn't time to do it and Mother didn't understand. My sister Joyce was too busy with her education, so it fell to me. Farmers' incomes had increased a lot during the war because of the need for food production. Before that time, farmers' tax had been paid on 'Schedule A', which was property-based and depended on the size of your farm. After the war, tax was based on 'Schedule D', which was to do with income. Accounts had to be provided if you were going to appeal against the tax office's decisions. One day, Father put a large brown envelope containing a lot of bewildering paperwork into my hands. He told me to read it and said that his accountant would give me some help.

Father's accountant was a wonderful man called Walter Johnson from Knutsford. I found out at an early age that when dealing with authority, it helped if you appeared to be a lot dafter than you actually were. This seemed to attract people's sympathy and they would try to help you. This was certainly the case with Walter, who seemed to take to me and understood the difficulties I was having. I went on to administer the PAYE at Yew Tree Farm for sixty years. If ever I found any difficulties with new tax policies, I insisted that someone came out to help me. After pleading the inexperience of youth, I was later able to plead the insanity of old age!

Dealing with Rats

Some aspects of farm life after the war were exactly the same as before. After the threshing you were left with the problem of rats. As their habitat and food supply had gone, they were desperate for food and would run around looking for prey, such as young ducks and hens. Just after the war, there wasn't any safe poison, so we tended to use other methods – chiefly shooting and ferreting – as methods of control.

Paralysed by Plaster

Our neighbour, Mrs Tunstall once used plaster of Paris mixed with sugar to get rid of the local rats. It worked because they couldn't resist the sweet taste and, once they went for a drink afterwards, the plaster of Paris set hard and that was the end of them! This method worked up to a point, but the rats kept dying in parts of the house where they couldn't be found. The smell was terrible, so Mrs Tunstall eventually thought better of her efforts and never used the plaster method again.

One night Father came up with a new idea about how to catch the rats on Yew Tree Farm. He had noticed that many of them were running out of a drainpipe in one of the pigsties where we kept ducks and his suggestion was that we put a sack over the end of the pipe and that I shine a storm light over the wall to entice the rats to come out. There were a number of problems with this method. Because the storm light couldn't be switched on and off easily (as a torch might have been), the rats got wise to our arrival. Also, on our first attempt, Father couldn't get the sack over the end of the drainpipe properly as there was only an inch of pipe protruding out of the wall. The rats were running all over his hands and arms and he thought that he would have to abandon the idea. We didn't want to block up the pipe as we knew that would force the rats back in amongst the ducks.

Our next idea was to get a piece of strong fencing wire and make a loop to fit over the pipe. We then threaded the mouth of the sack round the loop. This method worked better than the previous one, but the maximum number of rats that we caught at any one time was three. The trouble was that once the rats got into the sack, they would turn round and run right back out again. To stop this happening, I had to quickly twist the handle on the loop of wire to seal the entrance to the sack every time we had a few. This operation became a nightly one and enabled us to catch about thirty rats in all. Eventually an acceptable poison for rats and mice came on the market, but there were always some rats that wouldn't eat it and we continued to have to deal with them individually.

One day, Willie saw a rat in the shippon. It had disappeared under some steel plates that were part of the drainage system. Quickly, he blocked all the outlets and shouted to me for assistance. The idea was that he would lift up the plates, the rat would run out and I would kill it. The rat did run out but then disappeared again. I was wondering where it had gone, when Willie started jumping about and claiming that it had run up his trouser leg! At this time, most farm workers wore 'yorks' – a piece of string tied around the trouser leg just below the knee expressly designed to stop mice and rats climbing any further up. For some reason, Willie Moore had always refused to wear yorks – something that had always worried me a little.

On this occasion, I thought he was joking about the rat until, to prove his point, he bent down and I could see that there was a bulge on his bottom. I grabbed hold of it through his trousers and we struggled for a while. Had anyone been watching, we would have looked a very funny sight. The next minute Willie started to undo his braces and pull down his trousers. This was when I first realised that he wore long johns. They actually proved to be the saving grace of the situation. Without that kind of old-fashioned underwear, we could have had a very nasty situation indeed!

Threshing and Chaffing

After the war, we continued to thresh using steam engines. During this period, a chap named Bill Rogerson was the steam engine driver. He said that he came from 'the other side of the water', by which he meant the northern side of the Manchester Ship Canal. When steam engines were replaced with tractors, Bill enjoyed driving those as well.

Wherever Bill worked, he seemed to be followed by two ladies: Annie Wadsworth, who was short and middle-aged, and her tall, thin niece. In later years, I compared them to Hilda Baker and Cynthia. Annie worked on a casual basis on the local farms in the summer and on the threshing machines in the winter. She was known for cursing like a trooper and flirting with the men; she used to call Willie Moore 'Little Boy Blue' because he always wore a blue denim jacket and trousers. At Yew Tree Farm Annie used to work on the stack and her niece carried chaff. This was the dirtiest job of all, but a very important one. We used chaff for bedding the animals, particularly the day-old chickens and the brooding hens.

The chaff was very light and had to be blown into large hessian sacks with a fan. If you didn't get the sack off the shute quickly enough, it would overfill with chaff and the fan would get blocked. When this happened you had to release the chaff either by using a stick or by putting your hand up the shute. Either way, the result was the same: the chaff would get up your sleeve.

The Problem with Chaff

Those farm workers who wore long trousers or ladies' garments (like Annie and her niece) found that the chaff could get into some rather uncomfortable places. Fortunately, when I first started chaff carrying, I was young enough to still be wearing short trousers and any of the stuff that got inside my clothing came out around my legs.

In the late 1950s, Father and I realised that threshing machines were soon to be replaced with combine harvesters and we started to worry that we would no longer be able to collect chaff. In anticipation – and not knowing what else to do – we filled a garage with it for use in future years.

Colt Breaking

Another job that continued very much the same after the war was 'breaking in' the horses. I always thought that this was a harsh expression; really all it meant was training the animals to work. Horses needed to be led about on a halter from the time they were foals and, as they grew, they needed regular handling. To get them actually to work was a long and difficult process.

The Colt Breakers

There were a number of what we called 'colt breakers' in the area and they were all personalities in their own right. Each usually had a small farm, and their horse-breaking skills gave them an added income. The most famous colt breaker locally was Dick Willet from Toft. He was known over a wide area. Years afterwards, when his farm was converted into a small hotel, its organic restaurant was called 'Dick Willets'. We also once had a colt broken in by a man named Cakey Wright at Mobberly. His name came from the fact that he catered at Chelford market, and did farm sales. He and his sisters covered a wide area with their service delivering cups of tea, ham sandwiches and meat pies in the middle of the day. Unfortunately, the horse we got back from Cakey Wright didn't turn out to be a good worker.

In order that they might be broken in, horses had to be driven with reins. This meant that they had to get used to having a bit in their mouths. The bit was about an inch thick – it

Shire horses on a nearby Cheshire farm after a hard day's work, 1930s.

had to be big enough to ensure that the horses were aware that they had something in their mouths, but smooth enough that it wouldn't cut into their skin. The bit would be fastened to the head collar. Leather straps were fastened to the large rings at each end of the bit, and these were attached at the other end to a circingle (a broad leather band round the animal's girth). This would be held in place by straps that went under the tail – a device called a crupper.

The idea was that as the colt got used to the bit, the skin that was in contact with it hardened up. The harness would be put on every day for a few hours until the horse stopped playing with the bit. The straps were tightened up slowly until this was accomplished and the whole process probably took from about ten to fourteen days. This happened in a loose box. Alternatively, the horses could be turned out in a field where they would walk around on their own, nibbling at the hedges. They had to learn to walk about with their heads held up and the straps tight.

We had a young horse called Winnie who needed 'breaking in'. On this occasion, we decided to do the job ourselves rather than hiring in a local colt breaker. Father borrowed some harness from a retired breaker who lived at The Old No. 3 Pub at Little Bollington. We got Winnie on the move by fastening a rope to the head collar, not the bit, and walking her round in a circle. It was not long before we attached reins to the rings on the bit and started driving her about. You haven't got a clutch and a gearbox on a horse. She has to be taught commands: 'Gee Up' for 'Go', and 'Whoa' for 'Stop.' With one person leading her with the head collar, and the other driving with the reins, you say the command words at the appropriate time and give a backward pull on the reins when you want the horse to stop.

Shire horses pulling a scrubber board to break up lumps in the soil, 1930s.

Some Tips for Training Shire Horses

When training a horse, you need to make sure that you acquire a collar of the right size. It is important to remember that there is a difference between the neck and shoulder sizes in shire horses. You may think you have a found a collar that will fit, but you still have to get it past the horse's head. Fortunately, you can work this out by measuring the width of the animal's head between the eyes. This is the same as the width of the bottom part of its neck. Once you have got the right size, you put the collar on upside down, past one eye at a time. As soon as you get past the ears, you turn the collar the right way up. With a young horse, this is a difficult business and can take a long time. An older horse will usually just put its head through while you hold the collar, and then lift its head up, give it a shake and the collar will fly round into place. The collar for a horse has to be a good fit and in good repair. It has to fit back snugly on the shoulders. If it is the wrong size, or the padding is worn, the horse's shoulders will become sore.

The next step is to get the horse used to the hames chains. These have a habit of swinging about, jingling and hitting the animal's body and legs. It depends on the horse's reaction to this as to how long it is before you can attempt to get it to try to pull something. A log or something similar is suitable for the first attempts at work, because if things go wrong, there won't be any damage to the object being pulled. And, in the event of the horse turning or backing by mistake, there will also be little damage to the horse.

In training a horse, one of the most important factors to be taken into account is the animal's temperament, which is probably inherited. Until the modern methods of selection using production records, the shires used were mostly picked on the grounds of their physique and their show points. How quiet they were, or how good they were at work, were factors not usually taken into consideration.

Winnie made steady progress under our supervision and was soon working on a regular basis. However, we had a nasty accident in her early days of work. The first time she pulled a roller (a cylindrical barrel for flattening the ground), we knew, would be a test for her. Winnie had been harrowing some rough ground where the cows had been turned out for exercise in the winter months. I had sown some grass seeds and the ground now needed rolling flat.

The roller was in the stackyard. I put Winnie in the shafts and started to lead her by the bridle into the field. The yard was rough, and the roller started to make a loud banging noise. We started to gather speed. As we got through the gate into the fields, I tried to slow Winnie up, but to no avail. We started to go round in a circle and soon, we were back near the gate with a barbed wire fence looming towards us. I realised that we weren't going to stop and decided to save myself. I let go of the bridle and tried to throw myself clear of the roller. The result was that horse and roller went through the fence, and pulled up with the shaft of the roller on one side of a shed post and Winnie on the other side, held by the hames chain. The noise attracted some attention and Willie came to the rescue. Father also came out of the next field. Winnie was standing motionless. We got her untangled and Father took her back to the potato field, where he let her take the place of the other horse, David. We thought the best way to get Winnie over the traumatic experience was to get her straight back into work.

As for me, I realised that I had made a serious mistake in not driving Winnie with the reins. If I had been, I would have been behind the roller and would have had a lot better chance of pulling her up. At least by pulling on one rein, I could have run her round in a circle, till she was tired out. The upshot of this incident is that I ended up with an injured knee. Our local doctor was getting older and didn't listen to what I had to say about how it had happened. He just got it in his mind that I had been playing football and kept asking if the other fellow had been sent off!

The Harsh Winter of 1947

Living in the country, you learnt to accept the variations in the weather from year to year, but the winter of 1947 was something shocking and beyond my experience. It started to freeze on the 17 January and went on for three months with only a little bit of thawing here and there in the middle of the odd sunny day. There was a biting east wind blowing in from Siberia and near enough the whole country came to standstill. I'm sure that there was more snow on the eastern side of the country, but nevertheless, in Cheshire, we had a good six inches (which was more than enough) – and it had drifted onto the roads, making driving difficult.

It was a hard time for the animals. Every morning, we had to break the ice on the water trough in the old pasture field so that Winnie, who was still a foal at that time, could get something to drink. I also used to take her a bundle of hay, but she much preferred to push the snow off the ground with her muzzle and munch the grass. After a while, the wind blew a lot of the snow off the grass and short patches of sunshine melted it a bit. Thankfully, it was then no longer so difficult for Winnie to graze.

There were many electricity power cuts as a result of the weather. These didn't affect the farm too badly as, for one thing, we were still milking by hand. But there were other consequences. Our neighbour, Jack Wright, had just reconditioned our Allis Chalmers tractor but we didn't get to use it as it was needed at the Dunkerley's steel factory to drive an electricity generator. As it happened, it didn't really matter that we were without a tractor, because there wasn't much work for it at the time: the frozen ground was far too hard to plough. People from the factory came to collect the tractor one night after dark and we had a terrible job getting it on to the lorry that was to take it away. In fact, it was so difficult and dangerous that Father did the unthinkable and offered me a glass a whisky after our efforts in the snow.

A Farmer's Hands

Another effect of the weather was the state of my hands. In combination with the detergents that we were using at the time to clean the milking equipment, the cold caused them to crack open around the joints. I spent a lot of time at night covering the cracks with sticking plaster and this problem only really remedied itself years later when we obtained an automatic system for washing the equipment.

The Reluctant Midwife

In about 1948, a new neighbour came to live in Swiss cottage where Mrs Atkinson had once lived. Alan Pownall was newly married and was employed to work at High Legh gardens. He also had a great deal to do at home. The garden at Swiss Cottage was large and had been just grass for many years. The only attention it had had was when my goat Daisy had fed on it, or it had been cut for hay. But Alan was an enthusiastic gardener and was going to compete with his employers in supplying the area with roots and shoots.

Alan asked me to plough the garden at Swiss Cottage so that he could begin to plant it. The garden was rectangular, so it was a good shape to plough, but that was the only bonus. It must have been cultivated at some point in the past, but it had developed a thick turf with some big bogs of cocksfoot grass. This made it difficult for me to make a nice, even furrow. On the positive side, it was a good working soil, free draining and overlaying a gravel and sand bank (which must have been a glacier deposit from one of the ice ages). The A50 goes along the edge of this glacial deposit. Alan and I didn't plough up any of the boulders which are characteristic of the area that day but we did encounter plenty of tree roots.

The Mysterious Lime Tree

As I ploughed the garden at High Legh, I became aware that it contained a large lime tree that was unique to the area. Limes are not common in the open countryside. There are many such trees in local parks but these must have been deliberately planted at some point, probably in the nineteenth century. How this lime tree came to be at High Legh was a mystery. But, the answer might lie in the fact that the area (and indeed the A50 itself) was once an old coaching route, part of a Roman road network: all sorts of things would have been transported along it.

Alan's family – like his garden – was soon growing. It wasn't long before a baby was on the way. When the baby was due, we were the nearest people with a phone. It was understood that if anyone in the neighbourhood needed help, they should come to our farm. Alan came across one evening to ring for the midwife. But, on getting back to his wife, he realised that events had overtaken his planning. The baby was well on its way. Alan was soon back asking for Mother's help.

Apart from Mother, I was the only member of the family at home at the time. Mother didn't want to go on her own as she felt it would be quite a responsibility for her – being untrained – to help somebody give birth. Although she had had two children of her own, she said that she was no expert on births and she insisted that I accompanied her saying that I had had more experience of watching calves being born than she had. I did point out to her that my experiences with cows did not qualify me for midwifery, but she still dragged me along.

As we ran across the road, I was feeling increasingly terrified. My only hope was that Mrs Yarwood at Legh Cottage would be available. I knew that Mrs Yarwood's mother had been the local lady who was called upon to help at births and, as I ran, I calculated that she would have passed her knowledge on to her daughter. This made Mrs Yarwood a far more suitable person than me to accompany Mother. Much to my relief, Mrs Yarwood was at home and we pressed her into coming with us.

The three of us hurried onwards to the Pownall's cottage but I was still worried. To my immense relief, when we arrived we heard a baby crying. In the time it had taken us to cross the road and collect Mrs Yarwood, the midwife had arrived and the baby born. The panic was over.

Life in the Locality

When you live in the country – and by necessity away from other people – you realise how very important the local market towns are. Our nearest town was Knutsford about four miles away and situated on one of the main west coast road routes. For we farm types, Knutsford has always seemed a bustling, vibrant place with a good choice of banks, building societies, cafés and restaurants.

Bakers and Butchers

Most usefully for the farmers of Cheshire, there were shopkeepers in Knutsford who were prepared to deliver out in the rural areas. In the beginning, Mother used to shop at the Co-op. I think it was the 'divi' that attracted her. But she made a decision in the war years, when rationing came in, that she would be better off with a private grocer and she put her trust and her ration book in the hands of Alsops, an old established shop in Knutsford.

Alsops delivered once a week, collected the money and took the order for the next week. They always seemed to employ single girls who were hard working, able to drive of course, and who were responsible with money. I am sure that it wasn't the intention of these girls when they took the job, but their work soon became a marriage merry-go-round. Soon they

Our horse Winnie in the Knutsford May Day procession, 1958.

were showing off their engagement rings and marrying the eligible young men that they had met whilst out delivering their groceries. There was another grocer's in Knutsford, Watsons, which also had a bakery and which delivered bread, freshly baked with a lovely crust, two or three times a week. Of course all this was before the saying, 'Best thing since sliced bread.' I never agreed with this remark. In my opinion, you can't improve on freshly baked oven bread.

There were also several butchers' shops in Knutsford and most of them had their own slaughterhouse on the premises. These were family businesses and the skills of presentation and hygiene had been handed down over generations. Nothing was on as big a scale as it is now. This was a good thing in my opinion, as the scaling up has probably increased the risk of disease and infection. But these butchers – even without fridges or stainless steel – knew all about bacteria and cross-infection and kept their shops and slaughterhouses scrupulously clean. Like the grocers, the butchers would deliver out in the country areas to farms like ours. They would buy their cattle, sheep and pigs from the local farmers, or from the local livestock markets. As a result, butchers, I found, always knew the local rural area very well. If ever I was looking for a farm in another area, I always reckoned that the police, the post office and the people in the street probably wouldn't know where it was, but the local butcher would soon have you going in the right direction.

Okell's Chapel
Whilst most of the local farming fraternity attended the Church of England services at St John's church, High Legh, St Mary's chapel, High Legh, or St Mary's Rostherne, there was also an Independent Methodist chapel in the area. This was on Northwood Lane and it had originally been started during an evangelical tour by John Wesley in the eighteenth century.

St Mary's chapel, High Legh, which has been closed throughout my lifetime.

Okell's chapel, otherwise known as 'Okell's Meeting'. The Independent Methodist chapel at High Legh.

There is now a plaque explaining this under one of the M56 motorway bridges. The organ at the Methodist chapel was played by a local chap named George Okell and his sister Bessie. During the war, George Okell had been the star in the concerts at High Legh School. He sang the comic songs of the day, such as, 'When father papered the parlour,' and accompanied himself on the piano. George and his sister Bessie both played the organ: George played in the morning and Bessie in the afternoon at Sunday Services at St John's church. In the evening they would both be at the Methodist chapel. They were there so often, the place became known as 'Okell's Meeting.'

The Okells became outcasts from the local estate as tenants there were expected to attend St John's or St Mary's chapel, High Legh. Many people, however, preferred the Methodist chapel. The Okell chapel's hymns were Moody and Sankey as opposed to Ancient and Modern. I never attended the chapel myself, but Father reckoned that the services there were very impressive with George at the organ and the preacher with more than the usual helping of fire and brimstone. At Harvest Festival you could apparently hear the singing over a wide area.

In the Hands of the Lord

One of the local girls took her boyfriend, John Pennington, along to Okell's chapel one Sunday evening. That very night, the young man got the inspiration to combine the running of his farm with his religious activities. He was a remarkable fellow who, after his conversion, was later often seen at Manchester United games at Old Trafford, carrying a banner with the slogan, 'Jesus Saves'. John was also always in the procession at Knutsford May Day.

John's religious and farming activities sometimes didn't fit that easily together. When he went away on religious missions, he would leave a man in charge of the farm, and before he left, the two of them would discuss the priorities of what needed to be done. On one occasion the man asked John what he should do with the crop of swedes. John replied that the Lord would look after them. The man, thinking they needed attention, raised his eyebrows and said that he had not seen Him working with them lately.

Characters in the Local World

After the war, as before, some of the chief delights of my life were the numerous distinctive local characters, each with their own memorable personalities, behaviours and sayings.

Mrs Yarwood – The Guardian Office
People always think that those who live in the country must be cut off from the news. Nothing could be further from the truth. There are always certain characters who can be relied upon for information. Our neighbour Mrs Yarwood was one of these. She was known in the village as a lady who 'does' – that is she 'did' cleaning and general household chores. She was honest and reliable, everybody knew her, and she was interested in all their activities. She had several friends of the same disposition and they all met up in Mrs Yarwood's kitchen which was known by Uncle Frank as 'The Guardian Office'. Since Mrs Yarwood helped my friend J.P.'s mother two days a week, both he and I were always kept informed of the local news. In fact, J.P. often referred to Mrs Yarwood as 'Reuter'.

Bill Brooks – Milk Carrier and Cynic
Another source of information were the milk carriers who went round the farms. They picked up the churns of milk, locally known as 'tankards'. The carriers all had different personalities

and each had his own method of lifting the tankards onto the lorry. One man that we had for years was very small. He threw the tankard up in the air and made sure his fingers on the bottom were well out of the way just in case the tankard missed and came crashing down on the side of the lorry. Otherwise, there was an awful mess. At the other extreme was Bill Brooks. He moved at a much more leisurely pace and his method of getting the tankard on the lorry was a slow lift. I think he was expecting any other person he worked with to be making a greater effort. Bill had his own cynical take on the world. To get a clean and hygienic product when you are milking cows, a lot of preparation is needed. Bill called it 'ceremony'. Sometimes when a farmer he knew had got up late, he would remark that there hadn't been much 'ceremony' that morning.

A Word On Politics

Bill Brooks was full of somewhat depressing home-spun wisdom. On election day, I asked him if he was going to vote. He said that he would, but not because he believed any of the candidates would do any good. The only thing you could do, he said, was 'vote for the one who would do you the least harm!'

Henry Wilkinson – The Daredevil

Henry Wilkinson lived near the Kilton Inn and worked on the threshing machines. He had a sort of wild enthusiasm for life and lived dangerously. When a threshing job was finished, or at the end of the day, the belt driving the baler on the threshing machine could be slipped off before the tackle was stopped, usually by pressing the handle of a pikel on the belt. The belt would then come off and could be rolled up. Once, however, I saw Henry try a different method. He jumped up and stopped the flywheel by hanging onto the spokes. The belt flew off over his head. The next time I saw somebody else – a contractor named George Barlow – using a pikel handle to stop the belt, I told him about Henry Wilkinson's method. Being young, I thought what Henry had done was acceptable. George explained that it had been a very silly thing to do – Henry could have been taken round with the wheel and badly injured or killed.

There was no end to Henry Wilkinson's tricks. It was reckoned he would tie parked cars together with an oily rope, in the car park of the Kilton Inn. On one occasion he was seen walking out along the steering arm of a tractor to adjust the radiator blind, while it was pulling a threshing set along the road.

Before he had a motorcycle, Henry rode to work on a bicycle. One day, he was trying to get to work on time – something that was hard to accomplish given his nocturnal activities. Flying along the A50, he managed to catch up with a lorry near the Whipping Stocks pub, tacked onto the slipstream and hung onto the back of it. He sped down Garlands Hollow, and kept in contact with the lorry right through Knutsford, past the police station, before negotiating Mere traffic lights. On nearing Henry's destination in High Legh, the lorry went over a bump in the road which caused the handlebars of the bike to slip under the back of the tailgate. Drastic action was needed. The lorry wasn't due to stop again until the traffic lights on the outskirts of Warrington and this would be the next opportunity that Henry had to disentangle himself. Realising this, Henry put the age-old emergency stopping method into operation – his feet. It proved successful and he broke away from the lorry and made the right-hand turn down Crabtree Lane. The only problem was that he had worn out a perfectly good pair of boots. He had probably travelled a distance of eight miles in tow.

Henry had other unusual methods of transport. The local farmer's young daughter had a donkey – a very affectionate animal that Henry realised would be easy to catch. This animal lived near the Kilton Inn and Henry got it into his head to make an entrance into the pub on

The Kilton Inn, Hoo Green, Mere. The pub was named after a famous racehorse. Legend has it that Dick Turpin drank here after he committed murder in Altrincham.

it. So that's what he did – riding it in through the front door and out of the back. Perhaps the local legend that Dick Turpin had probably stayed at the inn had inspired him. He certainly seemed to think that he was a modern-day highwayman.

Dick Spencer -The Fire-Eater

One untrustworthy local character was Dick Spencer. He was supposed to be the black sheep of his family and he certainly lived on his wits. His main occupation was tarring the Dutch barns on different local farms. For an increased fee he would ride a bicycle along the top of them. His favourite trick was to take a mouthful of petrol, blow out and put a match to it, sending out a burst of flame. He was once caught up to no good in the hen house of a farmer called Eric Shore. Eric wasn't a very big man, but he didn't call the police. He preferred to distribute the punishment himself.

Bert Shore –The Super Shot

Bert Shore was a travelling salesman for Manchester and District Farmers. A traveller selling to farmers, he first had to sell himself, gain the confidence of the buyers, make them aware of market trends and ensure the prosperity of the firm he represented. Getting the money in can't have been an easy task. Bert was a shooting man and sometimes bragged about his exploits. We didn't always believe him. One evening, he had – he said – positioned himself on the banks of a pond and was waiting for the ducks to come flying in to feed. It was going dusk and he hadn't had any success, when he suddenly heard a duck quacking out on the field. He looked round and saw a duck coming out of the gloom. He fired. On going to pick up the bird he apparently discovered six more had been walking behind it. He claimed he had killed seven ducks with one shot!

Peter Hewitt – The Honorary Yankee

Peter Hewitt was one of the workers at nearby Knowles Pitt Farm. He had been out to Canada and let you know about it at every opportunity. He certainly had some big stories. One evening, Peter came up to Yew Tree Farm to tell us about his exploits in Canada. I remember Mother was picking raspberries and I was watering them with a hosepipe. Peter chewed tobacco and spat a lot as he spoke. At the end of every sentence he would spit. He stayed so long that evening and spat so much that I don't think my efforts with the hosepipe were needed. So often did Peter talk about life across the Atlantic that my friend Joe Whittaker referred to him, somewhat inaccurately, as 'that Yankee B★gger'.

The Man from Buffalo Bill's Circus

Local farmer Ted Whittaker had a man helping him who lived in a hut on the football field at Knutsford. Helping Ted with the harvest was this man's way of paying the rent, but his main job was haystack cutting. I remember him riding past on a bicycle, grumbling to himself, with a hay knife tied to his crossbar. The interesting thing about this chap was that he reckoned he had cut stacks of hay for Buffalo Bill's Circus, when it was on its European tour. The circus came to Manchester and Salford in 1887 and in 1903, so it was just possible that this elderly fellow was telling the truth.

Ted described how once, when his men were finishing the harvest, they had had a tall crop of oats which had nearly all gone flat and had to be cut one way with the binder. Whilst the workers had stopped for 'baggin,' the man advanced a theory as to how the oats had been flattened – he said that perhaps it wasn't the wind and the rain after all, but the elephants out of Buffalo Bill's Circus!

King Street, Knutsford. (courtesy of Cheshire and Chester Archives and Local Studies)

FIVE

The Young Farmer

After the war, I started to spread my wings a little. As a child, I hadn't been away from Yew Tree Farm on many occasions. Mother had sometimes taken me to see the George Formby films at Lymm cinema on a Saturday afternoon, but in my teens, I went a bit further afield and started to cycle to Knutsford with my school friend Pete Ford. There was often a Western on at the Marcliff – a new purpose-built cinema.

The cycles were in good order and just needed new lamps. When Mother and Father had ridden them in the early days of their marriage, they used oil lamps but, by the mid-1940s, these were completely out of date and were unreliable, especially in windy weather. Pete and I joined up on our cinema trips with another boy called J.P. who was about two years older than us. I once found myself at the bottom of a roadside ditch after giving J.P. some cheek. I think this must have cemented our long-lasting friendship as we became bosom pals afterwards and went everywhere together.

Flying the Nest

While feeding the calves, I've often watched fledgling swallows lined up on the beam their nest is built on ready to fly off. I've watched their parents bringing them food, but also enticing them to fly by hovering about a foot away. If they don't venture out and learn to fly by themselves, young birds do eventually have to be kicked out of the nest by their parents. I needed no such encouragement to spread my wings when the time came.

The Knutsford Young Farmers' Club

My childhood heroes were the local Young Farmers' Club. As a boy, I had been taken to the Cheshire Club's Ploughing Competition held at Fryer's of Wincham. It was a great success with a thousand people attending and a cheque for £200 being presented to the Red Cross. I remember that the whole family went along and I had the day off school in honour of the occasion. But it wasn't until I left school in 1945, that the – more local – Knutsford Young Farmers' Club (KYFC) came properly to my attention.

There were sixteen Young Farmers' Clubs in Cheshire at that time, all operating on the same basis. Now that we were older, my friends Pete, J.P. and I wanted to join the KYFC properly. We attended a stock-judging competition on a nearby farm with my father and were very nervous about presenting ourselves as would-be members. We needn't have worried. The chairman of the Knutsford branch was an excellent ploughman named John Greenway. The treasurer was Ted Bowen and the secretary was Frank Woodhall (who had held the position

Aged twenty-one in 1953.

since 1937 and was very much in control). When Frank saw that we three boys wanted to join, he shouted, 'Now you lads,' and we got down to business. I had entered the competition and went home that day with the Cowburn cup.

I don't think that Mother was too keen on the idea of me joining the Young Farmers' at the age of fourteen. They had quite a reputation and she thought that I might get led astray. Frank Woodhall must have been aware of mothers like mine as he never organised meetings or events in licensed premises. In time, Mother relaxed. I think she could see that belonging to the Knutsford Young Farmers' Club was educational as well as enjoyable, not least because so many of the other members were students from the agricultural college at nearby Reaseheath. At that time, very few farmers' sons went to agricultural colleges. Strange as it may seem, most of the students at agricultural college were new to agriculture and often ended up working for corn merchants or fertilizer and spray manufacturers rather than on farms. But, as fellow members of the Young Farmers' Club, these people, along with the staff and lecturers from the college, and the field officers from the Ministry of Agriculture, were invaluable to our education.

The Root and Fruit Show

In the 1950s, one of the Knutsford Young Farmers' Clubs best-supported events was the Root and Fruit Show that was held every October in the Church Hall in Knutsford. The hall would be filled with the products of the year's labour. This was before the silage revolution and the demise of the threshing machine, when cattle were still being fed on interesting items like mangolds, swedes, cabbage and marrow stem kale. All of these crops made an appearance at the show.

Kale was widely grown, but not popular with those of us harvesting it. For the cattle to eat it, it needed to be fresh every day. But as it was early winter when we were collecting it, the crop was often either frozen or wet. Kale could grow up to 7ft tall and would be blown about by the autumn storms. Harvesting it, therefore, was like going into a jungle. We would cut it off (using an implement similar to a machete) just about six inches above ground level where the stem became succulent. Transporting a fully-grown stem to the church hall for the show was a big problem. Sometimes, I used the Morris 8 with the leafy part of the plant sticking out of the sunshine roof. Care had to be taken that the foliage didn't snap off and end up on the windscreens of the vehicles behind!

At the Root and Fruit Show of 1952, there were twenty-eight individual classes including four classes for bottled fruit. Bottling was the only way of keeping fruit in those days. Grain was judged in bundles of fifty heads of oats or wheat on 12ins of straw (rather than whole sheaves). It was stipulated that all produce had to be home-grown and this rule applied to all classes. In the case of mangolds, better meant bigger. Consequently, in the weeks before the show, the countryside was full of young men scouring the fields looking for the biggest examples they could find.

Days Out

As well as local events, the Knutsford Young Farmers' Club organised a varied mixture of interesting days out. These were our further education – the way we found out how the rest of the country lived. We visited many places, including the Massey Ferguson Tractor Factory at Coventry. This was the largest tractor plant in Europe and some local boys were even employed there in various jobs.

We also visited Bournville, the village set up by the Quaker Cadbury family. After going round the chocolate-making factory that day, we young lads sat in the canteen enjoying some biscuits and hot chocolate. J.P. had the temerity to suggest that our lady guide didn't really know the Cadbury family personally. The guide was most indignant, saying that she did indeed know a number of the family and she asked us if we had noticed a young girl who had been observing the tin-can making machine. As full-blooded males, of course, we remembered her. This pretty young thing was, apparently, the latest member of the family to come into the business. According to the guide, it was the company ruling that each family newcomer had to work on each process in the factory for two weeks. The next Christmas, we were delighted to see that one of the Cadbury selection boxes featured on its cover the very same Miss Cadbury that we had seen that day – with a horse.

On all these excursions, it was interesting to see other people's conditions of work, from the steel rolling mill at Shotton (reckoned to be one of the longest of its kind in the world), to Bradford Colliery in Manchester, which was probably the most modern mine in the country at the time. Sadly, many of these operations – some of them very successful businesses – have since closed down.

Dancing

The Young Farmers' Club was always coming up with new ideas for entertainment. During the early years of my membership, the Angel Hotel in Knutsford was refurbished and the KYFC were the first organisation to use it for a fancy-dress ball. I remember that the winners were Jim Gough and Arthur Leech who had turned up as the Bisto kids. How their truck with its iron wheels was tolerated on the polished dance floor, I'll never know, but it begs the question whether the management actually knew it was there.

We enjoyed ourselves at these events, but it became obvious that none of us could dance. On realising this, the local matriarchs must have got together and consulted. They were unanimous that their sons (and indeed their daughters) should learn ballroom dancing. I had nothing against any pursuit that meant meeting up with girls (indeed, girls dancing in any form were very acceptable to me), but the thought of men dancing didn't really appeal to me. J.P. and I considered the situation, however, and came to the conclusion that if, at some time in the future, we wanted to achieve married status, it was a sacrifice we would have to make.

And so it was that along with many others from our age group, my friends and I assembled in the Church Hall in Knutsford where we were professionally greeted by our instructor – Peggy Hope. This was a pleasant surprise – she was a very attractive young lady and said that she was going to teach us how to 'trip the Light Fantastic'. Soon something that we had anticipated as an ordeal became a pleasure. Peggy taught us the Modern Waltz, Quick Step, and Slow Foxtrot. The old-fashioned (or Viennese) Waltz was also required because it featured in other dances that were popular at the time – the Valita, the Doris Waltz, the Pride of Erin and the Military Two Step.

I sometimes fancied that Peggy was giving me preferential treatment as she seemed to single me out. Looking back, my dancing was so bad I can't possibly have been the teacher's pet. It's more likely that Peggy saw me as a challenge! In recent years, I have heard an Irish song that reminded me of the difficulties I had in those days learning to dance. It goes, 'His left foot was lazy, his right foot crazy/Don't get uneasy, I'll teach you to dance.' With Peggy, I could soon waltz both forwards and in reverse – something I have found difficult to achieve ever since. Towards the end of our evening's tuition, to my disappointment, a tall man would always appear to look after Peggy. He worked for the Manchester and District Farmers, so I reckon that he knew that he had to keep an eye on eager young 'agricultural types' like me.

Dance Hall or Shippon?

Some of the members of Knutsford Young Farmers', especially those from nearby Mobberley, were more familiar with the Victory Hall in their own village than with the Angel in Knutsford as a venue for dances. At that time, milk production was being encouraged, and farmers all over Cheshire were putting up new buildings to house extra cows. On entering the ballroom at the Angel, two dairy farmer's sons from Mobberley once remarked in all seriousness: 'it would have made a bloody good shippon!'

Characters at the Knutsford Young Farmers' Club

There were a number of outstanding members of the KYFC in my time. One of the most respected was Jack Hamlyn. He worked for the Fertilizer Division of Imperial Chemical Industries. Jack knew how to make any plant grow. He didn't just advocate using artificial fertilizer but also extolled the benefits of farmyard manure and crop rotation. Luckily for him, he talked the same language as we farmers – it was the only way somebody better educated would be accepted by us lesser mortals. Jack went on to be a stalwart of the Cheshire Show Society and so remained in contact with the agricultural community.

Another respected figure in the Young Farmers' was Dr Ken Walley. He was of farming stock and had studied animal medicine at Cambridge University. He and his wife came to live in Knutsford and it was then that he got involved with the club. He was a great help in the educational competitions because of his wide knowledge of farming, animal husbandry and public speaking. After he left Cambridge – where he had stayed on as a lecturer for some time – he worked at Alderley Park, the animal medicine division of I.C.I. One of his duties, apart from the animal side, was to supervise the farm.

Ken had a strong personality and a sense of principle. There was once a conference on at Alderley Park about the hierarchy of the organisation. Ken hadn't been invited and wasn't very happy about being overlooked. It was apparently a very hot summer's day and all the windows in the conference facility were open. Suddenly, whilst the conference was in full swing, the delegates realised from the smell that muck spreading had commenced outside the window. This continued throughout the day. The next day, Ken was called in and asked to explain the situation. He had taken his diary along as an alibi. When he opened it at the appropriate page, lo and behold, the words 'muck spreading' were written across it, as if the whole operation had been planned months in advance. There was nothing anyone could say.

Ken was excellent at tutoring us in our debating competitions, offering us the hospitality of his home while we practised. His wife Pat would sometimes sit next to me and she often came out with some very witty remarks. Once Ken was pontificating about controlling poultry with an electric fence. I gave a gasp as I hadn't heard of this before. Realizing I was amazed, Pat said she was concerned the result of this new technology might be a field full of prostrate hens awaiting artificial respiration!

Cheshire Cowboy

At one of our meetings, Ken mentioned the cowboy style of roping animals. His wife Pat leant across to me and asked whether or not I could 'make a lasso.' I retorted cheekily that I probably could but not in the way she meant!

Ken was appointed as president of the Knutsford Young Farmers' Club in 1956 and held the office for ten years. Clubs still compete for the Walley cup every year in inter-club debates. He was later elected as the Independent Member for Knutsford on Cheshire County Council. Quite often his vote held the balance of power at County Hall.

Lady Members

I have often thought that change sometimes comes about because of a mistake that has been made and, in a way, it was because of a mistake that the Young Farmers' Club ended up accepting lady members. In 1952, we had a new secretary, Frank Williamson, and a dance had been organised at the Victory Hall in Mobberley. When we arrived, there was one thing missing – the caterers. It was customary to have an interval at about 10 p.m. for refreshments and Frank assured us that he had booked the usual catering firm, but as the evening went on, they didn't arrive. We contacted the firm and they said that they had a wedding in the family and had completely forgotten our booking. However, after discussion, they said that they could supply us with tea, sugar, biscuits and whatever they had in cakes.

We men were all in a bit of a panic. Somebody went off to collect the provisions and Bill Leech who lived nearby went home for milk. The rest of the club hierarchy began to fill the boiler and got the cups and saucers assembled. None of us really knew what we were doing. One of the members, Geoff Gough, came into the kitchen to offer his expertise. As we were sorting the teapots out he said, 'You don't need those, let me know when you are ready to brew.' We duly sent for Geoff. He put all the ingredients for making tea into the boiler and stirred the contents with a plate – Army style. The cups were then paraded under the boiler tap. We realised that we would have to start the washing up quite early on because there was a shortage of crockery. I was delegated to this task – something which for me was an entirely new vocation. Mother and my sister Joyce always did these tasks at home. On being asked where the clean crockery was, I pointed at the rack, only to realise that I had made a very bad job of it. Eccles cakes have very adhesive qualities and there was a currant stuck to one of the plates! It wasn't until near the end of the dance that we volunteer kitchen staff ventured on to the dance floor. We told the female guests what have happened and they assured us that they would have helped if only we had asked. The idea of having ladies as members of the club suddenly started to seem more attractive!

All this coincided with a time of national change in the membership of Young Farmers' Clubs. Some were already including ladies in their competitions, and the Cheshire Clubs were certainly already thinking along the lines of female membership. In 1952 the Knutsford club reorganised its committee system: the old idea of having a member from each parish was scrapped and, in its place, came the idea of a general committee including lady members and a social secretary. Doris Goostrey was the first lady to hold this position. Things were never the same again. For one thing, Ken Walley always said that having lady members made a difference to how he worded his speeches – this was especially true when he was talking about animal husbandry!

Over the years, Young Farmers' Clubs have been very good at raising money for charity and the lady members, in particular, have been instrumental in this. At Knutsford, Doris Goostrey had a social committee of lady members who baked and helped – not only at our Saturday dances, but also at our annual 'Fur and Feather' Whist Drive. We arranged whist drives to raise money for club funds because we were struggling financially. The whist drives were an excellent way of bringing in money, but our egos were severely bruised by the sarcastic tongues of Knutsford's expert card players. In later years, we held the drives in Plumley, which was a great success. Past secretary Frank Woodall was in his element as master of ceremonies. The prizes were a feather (that I don't think was bigger than a cock chicken's) and fur from a rabbit.

The KYFC club was very soon in profit and, under Doris's supervision, was running a Christmas draw. This was a good money-maker, held annually, with the proceeds going to various charities. Next we decided to depart from normal arrangements and hold a Saturday night dance at the Angel without refreshments. Other local organisations were apparently holding such events very successfully. Frank insisted that we needed an upmarket band with at least ten players, something different from the usual maximum of five. A lot of people smoked at that time so, it was said that Knutsford Young Farmers' Club had upgraded from 'a packet of Woodbines to ten Players!' Financially, the dance was a great success. We were able to charge five shillings instead of three shillings and sixpence (which had included refreshments) and the Angel was full. At first, nobody – including the Club Treasurer – seemed bothered about how many people were packed into the hall.

But, all good things must come to an end. Eventually, the management of the Angel became concerned about the numbers attending these dances because they far exceeded the maximum imposed by the fire officer. That was the end of the large dances, but Knutsford Young Farmers' Club continued to use the Angel for their harvest and spring balls.

Human Potatoes

One of the problems at the Angel was that the main entrance and exit was a revolving door at the top of steps onto the road. This was actually a safety hazard but because there had never been an accident, we young farmers used to joke about it, comparing the door to a potato-spinner which propelled people – rather than potatoes – out onto the street.

Local Entertainment

The Hops

As well as the Young Farmers' Dances, there were also plenty of more informal dances or 'hops' at which local bands played. Often these were held expressly to raise money for good causes. Hops were often held in the village halls, but my friends and I also visited larger halls such as the Regal at Alderley Edge, the Sale Locarno and the municipal halls in Altrincham and Warrington. Occasionally, we attended much larger events at the Winter Gardens or Tower Ballroom in Blackpool with entertainers such as Joe Loss and his orchestra. We used to refer to the local bands as a 'dead loss', but this was in jest as we actually got more pleasure from the hops than we did from the larger events. The dances were mostly respectable enough to ensure that those local parents who attended the Methodist church need not worry too much about letting their daughters attend.

Dead Give Away

Wherever we went dancing, we could tell straightaway which girls worked on farms. Even with their finery on, and even if they wore nylons, you could see the marks their wellies had made on their legs just below the knee!

The music at these local dances was called 'Popular' at the time, although now it would be referred to as 'Country'. There were some great musicians playing at the local hops. The village of Rostherne had the Kershaw family (David Kershaw played with the Bert Grange Band). There was also a chap named Len Ward who played many instruments and knew the steps to most dances. He would come down on the dance floor to demonstrate them. There was also one lady musician – Cath Jones – who had a tremendous following in parts of Cheshire. Cath had a music shop in Sandbach and was, therefore, always aware of new songs and tunes. On many occasions, she played them just as they were becoming popular. I remember that the Gay Gordon was a popular dance at the time. One night I asked why she didn't play the tune to 'Scotland the Brave'. She asked whether the steps to the Gay Gordon would fit the music. I replied that they did when Jimmy Shand played it. This was the inspiration she needed. The next time she played 'Scotland the Brave,' I danced the Gay Gordon to it!

The Adelphi Café

Another local place for entertainment was the Adelphi Café at Tabley. This was really nothing more than a wooden shed and it served many purposes. In the daytime, it was used mainly as a transport café but, as it was on the way to Pickmere Lake (a recognised playground for the people of Manchester), it also catered for cyclists. A plaque of the Cyclists' Association was proudly displayed outside. In addition, the local Women's Institute sometimes held their meetings in part of the café area. When I knew the Adelphi, the proprietors were Mr and Mrs Jones. The Joneses lived in Knutsford, where they attended the Methodist chapel and were very well respected. Mr Jones was seldom seen and seemed to control the kitchen area. Mrs Jones, on the other hand, was very much in evidence. She was always demurely dressed, her hair rolled into a bun and secured in place with hairpins. She had a warm heart, something that endeared her to people in all walks of life.

During the war there was a Land Army hostel about a mile away from the Adelphi. I suppose the matron there was impressed by the stature of Mrs Jones because she seemed to think that, under her supervision, the Adelphi was an ideal place for entertainment for the girls working on the farms. These young things had sometimes come out into the countryside from the big cities of Liverpool and Manchester and to them the country world seemed like a dangerous place. As one of them once remarked meaningfully to me, 'You country boys see life in the raw with the animals – and you want to act the same!'

I never went to Mrs Jones's entertainment evenings, but our gang did go to the dances at the Adelphi after the war. The tables were cleared to make a suitable dance area, but they were brought back for refreshment time. We always had a band supplied by a man affectionately known as Curly Webb (because he hadn't got a hair on his head). Curly was the drummer. The pianist was Mrs Oakes – a brilliant musician but a very unusual lady otherwise. I remember that she rode round Knutsford on her bike and created an extraordinary impression. She must have had an unfortunate illness earlier in life – perhaps polio – because she had one leg that was much shorter than the other. This seemed to be quite common years ago, but most of those afflicted with it had a wooden block bolted onto the appropriate pedal on their bike so that they could pedal normally. Mrs Oakes didn't avail herself of any modern inventions like wooden blocks: she just peddled with one leg. This in itself may not have been that spectacular, but her other leg would be protruding outward, and at the same time, she would fling her arm out and shout 'Oy!' I wasn't aware of Mrs Oakes's affliction being apparent when she played in the band – if it had been, it might have resulted in a new kind of dance.

Mrs Jones's Swear Box

The language of the truck drivers at the Adelphi could be a little rich. Mrs Jones, being the kind of upright lady she was, provided a swear box. When one of my acquaintance used a few words 'from the back of the Bible,' he had the swear box thrust in front of him and was told to put a penny in. He promptly obliged but noticed that there was a ten-shilling note already in the box. 'Hell Missus,' he said, 'somebody has done some cossing!' We always wondered after that whether the ten-shilling note was there because Mrs Jones had persistent offenders, or whether you could buy a season ticket for swearing in advance!

Unfortunately, the Adelphi Café was demolished when the M6 motorway was built in 1963. As the route of the motorway was planned, care was usually taken not to split parishes, but this was not the case with Tabley. Here the route was determined by the presence of a Grade I Listed Building, Tabley House, which of course had to be retained and protected. This resulted in a bend being created in the motorway with a service station being built at the southern end of the bend and Junction 19 being built at the northern end. There were a very high number of accidents because of the crossing and weaving of the traffic making the necessary manoeuvres. Junction 19 was built just where the Adelphi Café had been situated.

Holidays

Although the milking machine had made life easier, Father had hardly been away from the farm since he started milk production in 1934. Mother had occasionally taken Joyce and me to the seaside with our buckets and spades as children but otherwise we had stayed at home. As I got older, I felt the farm could manage without me if I took a few days off. There were two periods in the farming calendar suitable for summer holidays: the middle of May after the spring work was finished and late September after the harvest.

Ayrshire

In the early 1950s, my friend J.P. and I left Cheshire for Ayrshire to visit his aunt and his cousin Harry. This was a fresh experience, not only for us, but also for J.P.'s car at the time – the Ford Popular – which seemed to relish ascending Shap Fell. As farmers, one of the first things we noticed on that holiday was the difference between the Scottish cattle and our own. In Cheshire, black and white milking cows or Freisans had become the predominant breed, but here, it was the red and white Ayrshire. We were interested to learn that the Scottish farmers were ahead of us in the extermination of tuberculosis. More and more Scottish cattle were appearing in England at that time in an effort to help us get Attested Herd Status (i.e. a tuberculosis-free herd).

Whilst staying with J.P.'s aunt, we were not far from the coast and we were told to go and see sights such as Colzean Castle. General Eisenhower had a suite of rooms there which had been dedicated to him for his participation in the war. We also went to see the famous 'Electric Brae,' a slope which provides an astonishing optical illusion. Perhaps we were not as convinced as the locals about its disregard for the forces of physics but we had to admit that it was a great draw for the tourist industry.

While we were in Ayrshire, we came across an area called 'The Maidens' which is where early potatoes were grown for the Glasgow markets. J.P. and I were very impressed, especially because of our own rivalry in producing the earliest potatoes in our area. There is some light free-draining soil along the seafront in that part of Scotland which is affected by the Gulf Stream just as it is in Cornwall and Pembrokeshire. Thinking about this reminded us of what we would have been doing if we had stayed at home – probably hoeing the potatoes – just as the Scottish farmers were doing – or perhaps digging out docks and thistles in the oats and wheat.

London

In 1954, we were excited about visiting the capital for the first time. We were ambitious and decided that we could make visits to the annual Dairy Show in Olympia, the Motor Show at Earl's Court and several other tourist attractions. We had agreed that at our tender age and with our innocence, it would not be advisable to visit Soho, but we thought that the theatre known as The Windmill in Piccadilly would be an acceptable alternative. This seemed to be confirmed when, as we entered the building, we saw a family going in there with their young daughter. After watching some of the show, however, we were not surprised to see the father ushering the family out!

Staying in London was an experience for we boys from the country. The most startling aspect of it all was the prices. The Strand Palace was central and had a commercial section which had cheap rates. The first morning we were escorted to our breakfast table and asked what service we wanted. The choice was between à la carte, table d'hote and express raviers. The trouble was that we didn't know the difference between these and were reluctant to show our ignorance. In the end, we settled for à la carte and eventually the food appeared. There is an old saying which goes, 'It was all right, such as it was' – meaning the quality was good but the quantity was poor. We were young with ravenous appetites and had been hoping for a good start to the day. J.P. suggested that we buy a loaf to fill us up. We had also been recommended Lyons Corner Houses for snacks. Whilst we were considering our different options, we noticed some gentlemen of Middle Eastern appearance who seemed to have heaped up plates. Not only that, but they were making return journeys to the buffet bar for more food. We realised that 'express raviers' must mean something along the lines of 'self-service' – and from then on that was the option we chose. I remember that the attendant at the breakfast bar was a little alarmed at the amount of bread we were taking away each morning!

Hungry Lads

Young farmers always have enormous appetites. Later when I had two sons of my own working on the farm, Uncle Joe wrote knowingly in one of his letters from Canada, 'I guess you have no stale bread now!'

Blackpool

For holidays that could be fitted in with farm work, there was always the old favourite destination Blackpool – only about sixty miles away. With luck we would finish the harvest by Altrincham Show Day which was held in the 'teen days' of September. Legend has it that this is when 'Winter is at New Bridge Hollow' – the crossing over the River Bollin.

Blackpool supplied continuous entertainment at weekends or on week days when the weather was bad. The Illuminations extended the holiday season well into October, but, by then, we usually had to be back on the farm lifting the potatoes – and sowing the winter wheat. One of the small hotels in which we stayed in Blackpool was run by a lady called Gloria Swanson. She was a formidable and elegant lady, who in many ways resembled her Hollywood counterpart. Her claim to fame was that she was the president of Blackpool Boarding House Keepers and she certainly watched our comings and goings with an interested eye.

One of the unfortunate things about staying in that town was the possibility of catching the 'Blackpool Bug' – a particularly nasty type of sickness and diarrhoea. My friend Stan had it first. Mrs Swanson, noticed he was missing at teatime and, after enquiring where he was, suggested that she would go up and see him. This was the last thing we wanted. Stan was a practical joker. He was usually the first one in the bedroom and would leave the door slightly ajar. Invariably as you walked in something would come hurtling down – a suitcase or the waste bin. We were worried about what Mrs Swanson might encounter when she reached our bedroom. However, when she came downstairs again, she was just perturbed that Stan was rather poorly. It wasn't that we wanted Stan to be ill, but his sickness had probably saved her – and us – from an embarrassing situation.

There were things to do all day long in Blackpool. In the morning, you could visit Feldman's music publishers who advertised their wares by running singsongs of popular music. Stanley Park was a must in the afternoon for a row around the lake. At one time, our boat was just emerging from under a bridge when a large clod of earth suddenly descended onto the bow. We panicked, expecting that the next missile would score a direct hit. Getting clear of the bridge, we looked up only to hear a giggle and to see half of the social club of Knutsford Young Farmers' disappearing! We hadn't known they were there. In the evening, there would be least eight different variety shows to choose from with all the top entertainers performing. Dancing was available free if you went to a show at the same venue.

Because of our nocturnal revelry, we went to the circus in the afternoons rather than the evening. There were all the usual acts. The one that caused the most interest was the Unrideable Mule. A five pound prize was offered to anyone who could ride him. The animal wasn't very big and didn't look too dangerous a challenge. It was dispatched off round the side of the ring and members of the audience were asked to volunteer to ride it. You had to run around with it, grab hold of its short mane and jump on. The ring was covered with a very deep pile coconut matting, which thankfully assured you a soft landing. I made numerous attempts at riding that mule but never even succeeded in getting on its back. Every time I jumped on, the animal bucked and I found myself sitting on air doing a forward somersault and landing on the back of my neck. I watched carefully as other boys attempted the same feat and – being an observant type – noticed that when the immaculately dressed ringmaster

Guests, including me, outside a Blackpool guesthouse.

cracked his whip, the mule responded by bucking. When one of the circus hands demonstrated how to ride the mule, Mr Lockhart didn't crack his whip at all. After solving this mystery, we went back to our digs. We hadn't won any prize money, but we were much wiser about the ways of the world.

There were always further high jinks when we got back to Mrs Swanson's, sometimes on the part of the staff who could tell that we were game for a laugh. One night we sat down to boiled eggs for tea – something which struck me as a bit unusual. Suspecting something was afoot, we lifted the eggs out of their cups to find that the contents had been removed and they had been filled with mustard powder!

Courting

My friend Ted Whittaker was the most eligible bachelor in the neighbourhood and, in time, the inevitable happened and he met a lady whose charms he couldn't resist. On meeting up with him sometime after the wedding, I enquired how married life was. His instant reply was, 'Not as bad as I thought it would be!' This inspired me in my own quest for romance.

We Young Farmers travelled a wide area in our conquests but until I was in my mid-twenties, I had never been to Hilly Billy country – that is, the area around Macclesfield. This all changed in 1957 when a friend of mine, Prickle, reached the ripe old age of twenty-one and his mother invited us for a meal and supplied tickets for a dance in Macclesfield Town Hall organised by Adlington Young Farmers'. I had been through Macclesfield on many occasions, but I had never been inside the Town Hall. It was very impressive with a wide staircase up to the landing and a grand Assembly Room. In those days, it was no trouble to go up the stairs two at a time. In the ballroom, the boys, as usual, were seated on the same side as the entrance doors. The girls sat on the far side of a rectangular dance floor.

Young farmers out and about in Blackpool. I am the third from the left.

Hen in Red

We lads were always commenting to each other on the attractiveness of different girls. One night we had all noticed a pretty girl in a red pleated dress who had just settled on another girl's knee – all the pleats exactly in place. I thought she was exactly like a bird preening her feathers before settling for the night. I remarked to Prickle about the girl in red being 'All right'.

He said, 'You mean her that's just perched.'

That evening I met a girl called Kathleen for the first time and was smitten. The next morning I got the usual inquisition from my sister Joyce. 'How was the dance?'

'Great,' I said with a smile on my face. Joyce looked sceptical, 'Well, you won't be going there again anyway, will you?'

'Well yes, actually,' I said. 'We are going again – in a fortnight's time.'

'Not another Young Farmers' Dance.'

'No, Bosely church Restoration Fund.'

'Bosley church Restoration Fund!' scoffed Joyce. 'You wouldn't be seen dead at anything connected with High Legh church! What's going on? Mark my words, no good will come of this!'

The time of our lives: a Young Farmers' ball at the Angel, Knutsford. I am fourth from the right on the back row.

Kathleen came from Sutton near Macclesfield. Our relationship didn't get off to the most romantic of starts. When you are courting, you want to look your best, but soon after we met, I had the misfortune to catch ringworm on the side of my face. We had young heifers on the farm that had had the disease and I must have caught it from them. Ringworm is a fungus that usually comes around Christmas time when the days are short and there is no strong sunlight. It will usually clear up about Easter time when the days are longer and the sunlight stronger.

A Cure for Ringworm

There are many old remedies for this complaint, but none of them seemed to work for me. Ted Whittaker told me about his father's idea of using creosote to kill off the infection, but he wasn't very enthusiastic about it. He had apparently recommended it to an Irishman who was working for them who had ringworm in his arm. The creosote did eventually remove the ringworm, but it had also nearly removed the Irishman in the process!

After much discussion, the doctor referred me to Manchester Skin Hospital as he thought the ringworm was out of control. I received treatment with the most modern anti-fungicides but none seemed to have any effect. Whilst I was suffering, Father had slipped and split his elbow open and it had become infected. When the vet came to treat a sick animal at the farm, he was surprised to see Father with his broken arm and me with my face looking rather a mess. Just as Dr Hamlett had predicted, the hair cells on my face had become infected and I had come out in boils. The vet was very sympathetic and said that he was sure that both Father and I would have been better coming to him rather than to a doctor for treatment. He put forward Dettol (a disinfectant) as a treatment for the ringworm. I told the doctor at the skin hospital about the vet's suggestions, but he said he might face litigation if he recommended Dettol. By this point, I wondered whether it would really matter as my face was marked anyway, but I was getting pretty desperate by this point as none of this was doing any good for my developing relationship with Kathleen.

Eventually, I was spotted by a senior doctor at the skin hospital who was lecturing a bunch of students. He looked at my notes on file and asked the students for suggestions of a diagnosis. On being told I worked on a farm and must be 'affectionate' with cattle, one of them got it right. The doctor then put me on the oldest remedy he had, which contained sulphur. This finally seemed to work. On subsequent visits to the hospital as I got better, I suggested that perhaps the coming of 'Dr Green' (i.e. the spring) was helping. The doctor agreed and said, 'The Almighty also helps.'

Thankfully, my relationship with Kathleen seemed to blossom despite the ringworm! I think this was more due to my persistence than to her inclination. Kathleen's father was a master painter and decorator but really they were country people and a good living Christian family. Eventually I met her parents. Her father was a big man, tall and well built, with a wicked sense of humour and liked to watch my reactions to things. Kathleen had a strong resemblance to her mother. It wasn't long before her father told me a tale about a girl whose mother was the strongest personality in the household. When her boyfriend asked his prospective father-in-law for permission to marry, the father gave a hesitant reply and said, 'Have you seen her mother?' The boy said nervously, 'Yes, but I don't think your daughter will end up looking like her!'

Kathleen and I married two years later. It was customary for your friends to doctor the house for your homecoming after the honeymoon. We were no exception. When we got home we realised that a large bell had been attached to the inside door of our outside toilet. I'm sure that it could be heard all over Macclesfield every time we went! I still wonder about which of those many Young Farmers was responsible.

SIX

Characters From Home
and Abroad

After fifteen months spent in Macclesfield, Kathleen and I came back to Mere and I took over the running of the farm from Father. Whilst Kathleen and I lived in the main farm house, Father, Mother and my sister Joyce moved into a house behind the main farm building and we erected a poultry house for Joyce to keep laying hens in. Father carried on working on the farm but he wasn't paid a wage. He still owned the farm and the rent he received from me was his own private pension. He and Mother owned the house they lived in, and also had the state pension: they thought they were rich. Mother liked a day out at the seaside or a ride round the Derbyshire Hills. Father's idea of a day out was a ride around High Legh Moss in the next parish.

In the early years of our married life, Kathleen and I certainly weren't lonely. Some of the old characters were still about, among them were farm workers (some from the west of Ireland) and gypsies who parked their caravans in our fields. We were also entertained by the various visits of my uncles who had emigrated to Canada and who, over the years, I had heard so much about.

Tommy Bowker

Tommy Bowker was one of the workers who helped us on the farm at harvest time. He lived with his wife in nearby Burnt Cottages. Their home was a two-up and two-down and there was no electricity: Tommy didn't believe in it, saying that it was bad for your eyesight. But, of course, he didn't take into account the strain put on your eyes by trying to read by the light of a flickering candle or an oil lamp. The Bowkers also had an outside privy. Like a lot of people, they thought they were more comfortable than the indoor ones because of the wooden seats. This was true to an extent but, of course, there were always the pranksters who would sneak up to a privy silently, open the small door where the pan was taken out and push a holly sprig in. There were a lot of the old country people like the Bowkers in Cheshire in those days: they didn't want to get involved with new-fangled ideas.

Tommy's main job was as a roadman for Cheshire County Council. This helped to sustain his chief pastime – smoking. He picked up the butts of cigarettes – known as 'dimps' – from the gutter. These he kept in a lozenge tin, in the same way that a lot of people kept a pocket watch to keep it free of dust. When Tommy was in need of a smoke, he lit up one of these dimps. He had a moustache, a thick black one with grey flecks in it that betrayed his age and, because he only smoked dimps, he had burnt a mark over his top lip that had a reddish brown tinge to it.

Tommy and his wife lived a frugal existence. Mrs Bowker worked on a local farm along with Mrs Blake whose husband was Sam, the other road man. The two women spent all autumn and winter pulling what we call common turnips – a cash crop sown after early potatoes.

These particular turnips were small with a white flash. They were peculiar to Manchester and had a green top and white bottom and root. Mrs Bowker and Mrs Blake could be seen out in all weathers working from September to March. Only one thing stopped them and that was a very hard frost when they couldn't even kick the turnips out of the ground.

Tommy Bowker's Pearls of Wisdom

One of Tommy's sayings was, 'Never finish today what you could put off until tomorrow!' He also reckoned that you should never let a man stop a job once he had started it. He used to tell a tale about two men – one was digging out holes and the other one was filling them in. On being asked what they were supposed to be doing, they replied that there were usually three of them and that they were supposed to be planting trees but that the man who put the trees in the hole was off work ill!

Tommy had a number of mannerisms of speech. He used to mutter, 'He Hmm Hmm,' and he always called me, 'Young fella me lad.' He used to come and help us when we were short-staffed for important jobs in the spring and at harvest time. I remember once that we were hoeing the mangolds. It was a very wet summer and some wise old farmer (referring to the weather) said, 'You're either burnt out or drowned out.' Tommy said, with great emphasis, 'He Hmm Hmm. We've not been burnt out many times lately, young fella me lad.' This was very true as it was the fifties and there had been a lot of very wet summers.

Tommy helped us with the harvest. He wasn't lazy but he sometimes got carried away with his talking. I was in charge of pitching the sheaves in the fields on to the carts and Tommy's job was to place them in position to make a load that would transport safely to the stack yard.

Mrs Bowker and Mrs Blake at Hulme Barns Farm, Mere, picking potatoes, 1940s.

The main work depended on my energy in pitching the sheaves. I had to make sure that there were no thistles in the crop as Tommy would be using his hands (there were no sprays in those days and it was only gentlemen farmers who wore gloves). Tommy, like all farm workers, was trained in loading sheaves, so he was quite accomplished as long as talking didn't interfere with his concentration. I'm afraid he couldn't help himself, however. As he talked, his loads became more ragged and eventually part of a load slipped off. I knew we would have to move it as it had fallen in the grass field across which the cows came to be milked. This was late one Saturday afternoon and I had intended a visit that evening to the cinema to see James Stewart in *Bend in the River*. I was annoyed because films came late to the country: London got them first, then the major towns, and finally the smaller towns like Knutsford. As happens so often in farm life, however, work had to take priority. It was, in fact, about fifty years later that I finally saw that film on television.

Because they thought he hadn't got much, local people would joke with Tommy Bowker about what he was going to do with all his money. His answer was that he 'hadn't finished with it yet,' which gave the impression that he might be going on a world tour at some time in the future! This never happened, of course, but surprisingly it was reported when he died that he left a sizeable amount to Delamere church – in the area where he originated.

Irish Farm Workers

A lot of Irish men off the little farms in the west of Ireland came to work in Cheshire; some came to work on the building sites run by Wimpey and McAlpines but many took jobs on the local farms. The Irish workers were a tough breed of men. Hard physical labour was in their blood: their ancestors had been coming to the North West for years before to work on the building of the railways and the canals. Whatever they ended up doing, most of them came to work on farms first as this was the sort of work they were used to. Many had been 'hoeing swedes out of their prams,' as the saying went.

Nearly all the Irish workers wanted piecework and their speciality was lifting potatoes – a job they did with a fork. They were very good at it; many of them could use a fork with either the left or the right hand, so that they could 'get a drill' (as we called it) on either side of where they stood. This method was particularly good in wet weather. Getting potatoes out of the ground with a fork was a cleaner, quicker process than using a potato spinner.

The workers were paid by the score which meant by each twenty yards of ground they covered. They were supposed to lift all the potatoes and then sort out the smaller ones or 'chats' from the larger ones. Often they just didn't bother – and the chats would be buried. They worked long hours in the summer collecting potatoes in willow baskets called 'potato hampers' and then tipping them into in 1cwt sacks. I remember that one Irish worker, Jim Melia, filled fifty of these sacks in one day at the end of June one year. This said something about the early readiness of the crop, but it said a lot more about Jim's phenomenal work rate.

The Irish workers had a very basic way of life. They often lived in 'shants' or farm buildings which were hardly comfortable. They would get eggs and milk from the farms where they were working, but, for their rest of their needs, they would go into one of the local towns, Warrington or Knutsford, on Saturdays. Here they would buy bacon, cheese, bread, butter and beef which they boiled so that it would last all week. There was a lot of rivalry between them and it was all to do with who came from which part of Ireland. There were regular fights at the Kilton Pub between men from Galway and men from Mayo. But whatever had happened on a Saturday night, most of them would go to Mass on a Sunday morning.

Many of the workers had left behind a wife and family in Ireland and they would send money home periodically, sometimes in the form of postal orders. Of course, there were those who had forgotten their responsibilities and whose money went on fags during the week and beer at weekends. Some of them came back year after year to work on the same farm or in the same area; others moved from farm to farm without any warning. In fact, 'doing a moonlit flit' was quite a common practice. After all, the Irish were pieceworkers who were (in a way) self-employed, and they didn't want to pay taxes to the British government. The way they were paid came to be referred to as 'the lump.' Sometimes, the first a farmer knew of a worker leaving was when he found he was short of labourers on a Monday morning. Quite often the flitters told no one they were going and even the workers with whom they shared a shant were genuinely surprised to see them gone.

Some of the Irish workers met local girls, got married, grew wealthy, bought farmhouses in Cheshire and became part of the local community. One of these was a chap called Pat Kelly. I remember that the first time I met him he was wearing something unusual – an abstainers' badge. It was the first time I had seen such a thing and it somehow marked him out.

Pat was determined to make the best of his life. He started out living in the 'shant' at Bowdon View Farm – a building that hadn't been lived in for years and was in a bit of a state. People liked Pat and wanted to help him. Willie Moore, our farm worker, befriended him and set about making the place habitable with a bit of whitewash. Mother and Mrs Mason from the farm both took him under their wing and made him meals. Pat was always smartly dressed, so there was evidently someone doing his washing. He had an eye for the ladies and used to like going to the Irish clubs in Manchester at the weekend. He and I had this in common. I loved music too – although, in my case it was Country and Western music and Rocky Mountain Rhythm (in honour of my Canadian relatives). Some of my happiest times on the farm were when Pat and I, and another farm worker who could yodel, used to sing together in the fields as we were having our baggin'.

The Posh Gypsies

I had always been aware of the existence of gypsies. In my childhood, they would often pass the farm with their dappled horses and ponies and their exquisitely painted caravans. The men occasionally worked on the farms, but it was the women with whom we had most contact. They sold clothes pegs (probably made by the men) and were very persistent sales people. If the lady of the house didn't purchase, she would be rewarded with a curse that was meant to last until the next time the gypsies visited the area.

In the 1950s, there seemed to be a new, posher type of gypsy on the road. This lot had very big cars, large vans and enormous trailers which were well fitted out with kitchens and toilet facilities. Everything was rather flash – a lot of chrome was used in the construction of the trailers and in the accessories on the vans. I don't know whether they had bank accounts, but they certainly had a lot of ready cash. They would turn up at the farm door with a large bundle of bank notes about the size of a large toilet roll and proceed to peel off a number of sheets. What they wanted, of course, was to gain access to your land and be allowed to stay.

The particular group of gypsies who stayed on our land in 1955 were quite unlike the gypsies of hearsay and gossip. For a start, they were all very well dressed and respectable. The men went off in the morning. We never knew what they were doing and if we had asked, we probably wouldn't have been any the wiser. A police sergeant came up one day to interview them. Afterwards he came to see me and said that he had talked to one of their elders whom he referred to as 'King Pin.' Like me, the policeman had come away no wiser than when he had arrived about the source of the gypsies' income. The environmental officers from the local council also came for an inspection. Even they couldn't come up with any objection to the gypsies as the site was very tidy. In fact, these remarkable gypsies had even waylaid the dustmen and were paying them to call there!

There were two gypsy children of school age who went to the local school and I never heard of any problems with them. In fact, these gypsies were even members of the Caravan Club and had a Showman's Guild Card. When the fairground traffic was going past from Knutsford May Day, much pipping and tooting went on as they recognised their friends. While they were with us, our posh gypsies went to Royal Ascot and Doncaster for the St Leger. For gypsies, they were a very upmarket lot.

Compensation From King Pin

The only disagreement I ever had with the gypsies was over a part of a crop of wheat that had gone flat after a rainstorm. I complained to them that their dogs playing in it had rendered it useless for harvesting. Even then, I found them quite reasonable. I negotiated with 'King Pin' and pointed out some bones the dogs had left in the crop. After a long discussion, he eventually agreed to pay compensation. Soon after our disagreement, one of the other gypsies who had listened to my discussion with King Pin was washing his vehicle in our farmyard as they often did. He said that he reckoned I had made a fair challenge, and agreed that it was right that they should pay. After all, the damage had been done by their dogs.

Eventually we had to tell the gypsies that the council had begun to charge rates for land that was being used for business rather than agricultural purposes. We asked them to leave and made it clear that we didn't want them to return. After they left, we continued to get post for them. This included postcards stating that their dress suits were awaiting collection from Moss Bros!

Uncles

Three of my mother's brothers – John, Joe and Willy – had emigrated to Canada before I was born. They all corresponded with Mother, but other than their letters and a few photographs, we knew very little about their lives. I had been fascinated by my emigrant uncles for years, so when I got the opportunity to, at last, meet two of them in the flesh I was very excited.

Uncle John
In 1954, I got quite excited when a letter arrived from Canada saying that Uncle John was coming over. John had been the first of the brothers to emigrate. He went on the doctor's advice in about 1910 because he had rheumatic fever and it was suggested that a drier climate might be better for his health. He had been back once before, but I didn't remember his visit. When he arrived, I was quite surprised to find out what a quiet man he was. Some people might have said he was 'deep,' and, whether or not that was true, he was definitely not a good communicator. From a young age he had done things on his own. I was impressed by how much he knew about farming. I found out in later years that he had corresponded with a family called the Coopers in Suffolk in the thirties about the advances being made in grain farming in the Canadian prairies. This resulted in the Coopers being one of the first families in Britain to get a combine harvester in 1937.

On this occasion, the purpose of Uncle John's visit was to sound out the family about his possible return to this country. He wanted to know whether or not he would be accepted back into the family. There was a lot to consider. For a start, we wondered what Uncle John would make of the fact that his brother Frank was still running Old Farm mainly with horses. Surely he would soon realise that Cheshire was a completely different environment to Canada: a man used to the mechanised prairies was bound to be frustrated by our outdated farming methods. On top of these considerations, Uncle John's lifestyle was so different to ours. Over there, not having any horses to look after meant that he didn't have any winter chores. So, like a lot of prairie farmers, he would move into the large towns, or even go as far south as Texas for the winter. In recent years he had been through a profitable period, quite different from the dry, dustbowl conditions of the 1930s when some North American farmers didn't harvest a crop for three years.

Then there was the matter of space. Uncle John was used to having plenty of it. Back in Cheshire, Old Farm was a small house. Uncle Frank and their sisters Bertha and Gerty were

Uncle John sent this picture of himself from Calgary.

Uncle Joe and Uncle John.

not married but they had their own independent lives. The farm was no longer Uncle John's home. For all these reasons, it was eventually agreed – and thankfully by all parties – that it wouldn't be practical for him to return. So, after visiting some family members and other people and places that he remembered from his youth, Uncle John returned to Canada. Nobody really expected to see him again.

Some years later, however, in 1962, Mother got a phone call out of the blue from Warrington station. To her immense surprise, it was Uncle John. He had decided to make another trip over from Canada without telling anybody. Father went to pick him up while Mother got a bed aired. It turned out that whilst he had been over on the previous visit, he had met a lady on a visit to Kerridge, near Macclesfield. He had apparently been corresponding with this lady ever since.

Obviously, Uncle John wanted to visit Kerridge as soon as possible, so Kathleen took him up to Macclesfield where he got a bus to his destination. Later she picked him up at the bus station on the return journey. Apparently, he didn't say much. I suppose he had never met Kathleen before and, after all, he was a very quiet man. But he did talk to Mother later. He told her that the visit to the woman in Kerridge had been a complete mistake. He had been reading the wrong messages in their correspondence. The result was that he decided yet again to return to Canada.

Mother was very worried about this. Her brother Uncle Willy (whom I never met) was already living in an institution after leading a very lonely life on a prairie farm. Now Uncle John was returning to what appeared to be an equally lonely life. At least Uncle Willy received visits from Joe (the third emigrant brother). But Joe lived in the Winnipeg area which was 1,200 miles from Calgary where John farmed and, therefore, too far away for visits. There was a lot of anguish on Mother's part when Uncle John left that last time.

Uncle Joe
Every Christmas, Mother got her regular letter from her brother Uncle Joe in Canada. As time went on, something began to puzzle her: the letters started to contain more and more quotations from the gospels. Mother's sister, Auntie Bertha, also got an annual letter from Uncle Joe. In hers there was less news and more religion. She couldn't understand why there was so much theology. She remembered that Uncle Joe had gone to church when he lived in England and that he wasn't a thief or a robber. 'But,' she said with meaning, 'he wasn't a saint either.' When they had been younger, Mother had gone off to work for the Dunkerley family and Auntie Bertha would have been the eldest daughter left at home. No doubt, Uncle Joe tormented her. She had probably sighed with relief when he went off to Canada. Whatever the case, she wasn't ready to welcome and look after him if ever he came back to England.

Because of all this, when Uncle Joe announced that he was coming for a visit to Cheshire in the summer of 1964, Auntie Bertha said that she 'couldn't be doing with him' and didn't want to put him up at Old Farm. It would, therefore, be up to Mother to put him up at Meadow View, the house that had been built behind Yew Tree Farm. Father knew Joe because he had worked for him at Legh Oaks Farm before he went to Canada in 1919. When I asked Father what Uncle Joe was like he said that as a young man he had been full of exuberance but it had not always been directed in the right way. When Uncle Joe had taken the horses ploughing, for instance, the first thing he did was check his snares from the afternoon before. Father used to watch Joe's antics from the farmyard and would apparently let out a piercing whistle urging him to get on with some work.

I was very excited by Uncle Joe's arrival and was surprised to see that he was quite different from Uncle John. For a start, he was short for a Hulme, but what he lacked in stature, he made up for in personality. Having survived the dry years of the thirties, Uncle Joe had done very well in the better times of the war and post-war years. He had also been much more successful in his personal life than Uncle John and was married with four children. On the prairies, he was one of the few farmers who milked cows and he had roped his children in to help. There were other attractions about Uncle Joe too. I had heard – though I can't say from

Uncle John's car in Calgary.

Horses at the prairie farm in Calgary.

Uncle John's farmhouse in Calgary.

The quiet type – Uncle John came home in the hope of finding a wife.

whom – that the old goat was loaded. And then, of course, there was still the mystery of his religion to unravel.

At first, things didn't go very smoothly. Uncle Joe found the farm noisy. He was sleeping in the back bedroom near the henhouse and my sister Joyce's hens made a terrible racket laying their eggs. Like his brother John, Joe was used to the quietness of the wide-open spaces. It also turned out that Uncle Joe was a bit of a bragger. At that time Auntie Bertha had a Morris Minor in which she hared around the country. Uncle Joe, on the other hand, apparently drove a Ford Thunderbird in Canada – and didn't he let us know it! On seeing his sister's car, he exclaimed that he could probably fit it into the boot of the Thunderbird. After a while, I started to understand why Auntie Bertha had been so apprehensive about Uncle Joe's visit in the first place.

Father took Uncle Joe round his old haunts and to see the people he had known before he emigrated. He thought that High Legh had changed a lot, especially in the area where East Hall and West Hall had been. Now there were lots of houses in their place. He was surprised, however, to find that nearly all the farms were the same as they had been when he had left, as was St Mary's chapel. Uncle Joe told us lots of interesting things. We listened open-mouthed as he described how Canada and America had been surveyed with a compass and a tape

Uncle Joe in
Canada with
the infamous
Thunderbird car.

Aunty Bertha's
Morris Minor.

measure and how the land was split up into sections of a square mile (640 acres) and then split again into quarter sections. All the boundaries were straight, he said, with the divisions at perfect right angles, and nearly all the roads were straight apart from a correction line every twelve miles if you were driving in a northerly direction. He told us how the roads were built, with a shallow ditch on either side, and how the spoil from the ditch was used to make the road higher than the surrounding fields. The ditches ensured that there was somewhere for the snow to blow onto, or to be ploughed off onto. Uncle Joe also told us that he was a fast driver, and that he had ended up in one of these ditches just before he came over. This was why he had a bad shoulder.

Skidoos and Silver Foxes

Our two farm workers, David Okell and David Spruce, were both interested in talking to Uncle Joe during our tea breaks in the fields. He had known both their families when he lived in England and he liked to impress them with how well he had done for himself. One morning, he showed us all a photograph of a silver fox he had shot. 'Yeah, we go after them with the skidoos,' he said. We asked rather innocently whether 'skidoos' were some sort of fox hound – after all, Uncle Joe had done a lot of hunting as a young man. He told us that they were in fact motorised sledges on which two people could sit. It seemed that in North America, if you could put an engine on it and go fast in it, you did. According to Uncle Joe's account, hunting silver foxes involved catching up with the animal and holding on to its tail. I suppose we understood so little of Canadian life, that he could have told us anything and we would have believed him.

No change: St Mary's chapel, High Legh.

Whilst Uncle Joe was staying, Mr Beck our land agent had asked us to clean out a ditch out on the Capesthorne estate for which he was also agent. I needed to go and see how David Spruce was getting on with this task and it was opportunity to take Uncle Joe out for a ride and to try to impress him with how mechanised we Cheshire farmers were becoming. I was pleased that Uncle Joe seemed to be quite impressed with the ditching. He referred to the tractor-mounted digger we were using as a 'back hoe' – it was the first time I had heard that name.

As we were driving along, the Radio Telescope at Jodrell Bank came into view. Uncle Joe was assimilating the landscape and suddenly exclaimed, 'What's that?' After all his bragging, I couldn't resist. 'That's a pan to boil your cabbages in,' I said.

Just before Uncle Joe went back to Canada, Father took him to nearby Park Farm. The farmer there was my old friend J.P. and he had just started combining. J.P. was always very impatient and hadn't been able to wait to get going with his combine. I thought he was doing the wrong thing, because I thought the corn was under-ripe. I asked Uncle Joe's opinion when he came back. He said he thought that the crop was 'very tough' – by which he meant that the grain was soft and the straw under-ripe, as I had thought. He explained that in Canada, the whole process was totally different. The crop would be cut with a swather and left to dry until it was ripe. I asked him what he thought about J.P.'s combine harvester. It was a Massey Harris 735 – which was very small and I feared that he would find it very paltry compared with Canadian machines. But Uncle Joe said that a guy on a smallish farm near to him had one and that it was very successful. He sold his grain for seed. This made us all feel a lot better.

At that point, we still hadn't solved the mystery about why Uncle Joe had gone all religious. But, all was about to be revealed. Apparently, it was common in Canada to source your own water supply. On the prairies, that meant digging a well. This would be a two-man job with one man digging and the other man hauling up the spoil with a bucket and windlass. Wells had to be dug deep until a water-bearing stratum was reached.

Apparently, Uncle Joe and his partner had been making good progress when they struck a layer of rock about 60ft down. This brought operations temporarily to a halt. They purchased some dynamite, and Uncle Joe went down into the well to fix it in position and to light the fuse. As he was climbing back up to the top of the well, he got his foot entangled in the windlass rope, lost his balance and fell back down the well. The dynamite had ignited and he met the blast as it came upwards. His mind went completely blank. Eventually, he heard a cry from the top asking if he was all right. It was a voice he knew and not, thankfully, St Peter, whom he had expected. His friend worked the windlass and got him back up to the top. After this shocking episode, the two men, remarkably, carried on with the job, got through the layer of rock and found water.

This experience had profoundly changed both men's lives. Uncle Joe's partner had been so moved that he went into the ministry. Uncle Joe himself, realising what a lucky escape he had had, became much more religious. This accounted for the change that we had noticed in his letters.

I had enjoyed Uncle Joe's visit. He wasn't a forty-niner involved in the gold rush, but he had endured the difficult years of the 1930s and in my eyes he was a pioneer. Even Aunty Bertha said that he had mellowed a bit. There was no comment from Uncle Frank. Aunty Gertie got an invitation to visit him in Canada. Mother was disappointed that, as Uncle Joe's host, she had not been invited. She wouldn't have gone, she said, but it would have been nice to have been asked. Uncle Joe had his wife, Auntie Viola, and four children to return to. Unlike when Uncle John left, there were no tears from Mother when Joe went back.

SEVEN

The Centre of
the Universe – Chelford Market

At my friend Norman Sutton's funeral in 1999, the Revd Canon Noel Rogers commented that he loved to visit the 'centre of the universe - Chelford Market.' Those of us in the congregation who farmed in Cheshire and understood the importance of Chelford knew exactly what he meant. Situated just off the A537 Knutsford to Macclesfield road, Chelford Market was started by Frank Marshall and J.P. Haworth in 1947. Both men had originally worked for John E. Braggins auctioneer and estate agent. When Mr Braggins retired, he split the business so that Frank Marshall had the auctioneering side and J.P. Haworth had the estate agents including land sales. They both prospered.

You can, and always could, buy and sell almost anything at Chelford from hay and straw to cattle, fowl and other animals, and machinery. It was always full of produce from Lancashire, Yorkshire, Wiltshire and Worcestershire as well as from local farmers. There were loads of all sizes from large articulated 40ft trailers, six-wheel lorries and trailers carrying over twenty tonnes of hay and straw, to the other extreme – a small pick-up perhaps with a trailer 'loaded to the gunnels' behind. For many years, Chelford's attractions also included a large hardware and feed store and a butcher's shop. Liquid refreshment could be had at the Dixon Arms and good food at the canteen run by Cynthia Dale. While you were eating your dinner, you could catch up with the news from over a wide area.

Even in the past, the distances people travelled to trade in Chelford were remarkable. Years ago, I remember, a wagon came all the way from Aberdeen with a load of either turnips or straw. The owner bought calves, went out to deliver his produce to some local farms, returned to the market to pick up the calves and went home again that evening. This feat was even more remarkable when you consider that it happened before the motorways were built. The Wright family was lucky: Chelford was just twelve miles away from Yew Tree Farm. The first time I went to the market was when Father decided that our surplus straw, hay and mangolds might make a better price there than we could negotiate ourselves.

Hay and Straw: Sales and Deliveries

Chelford Market was one of the first markets in the country to sell hay and straw. In the early days it was sold by the bale with no indication of its weight. In theory, the big wire-tied bales would weigh between 100lbs and 112lbs. It wasn't long, however, before the auctioneers insisted on the bales being weighed because an industry had developed where farmers and straw dealers were buying heavy bales and then re-baling them and returning them as lighter and more numerous bales and making an inordinate amount of profit. This was a practice that didn't last long, as news soon got around the market about who was responsible. In general, I could never understand the variation in prices at Chelford: all markets rely on the laws of supply and demand, but also it seems, on the whims and fancies of the buyers on any given

Selling dairy cattle at Chelford Market in 2007. The auctioneer is Jonathan Farrell; the vendor is standing next to him.

The canteen at Chelford Market as it is today. Pictured are farming friends from Agden, Heatley, Siddington, Sproston and Dutton. My wife Kathleen is in the centre.

Selling bales of straw at Chelford in 2007, under the eye of auctioneer Alan Lane.

day. Nevertheless, the market was still, on the whole, the best way of marketing surplus straw and other produce.

For me, a trip to Chelford Market to sell hay and straw was a good day out – something of a holiday from the farm – particularly if, after selling my goods, I ended up having to deliver them beyond the market, to places such as Derbyshire. Many of the hill farmers who come to Chelford are 'hobby' farmers by necessity rather than by choice. This means that their land doesn't yield enough to make it a self-supporting business and they have to have other sources of income such as driving trucks or working in the quarries. I always found the Derbyshire farmers very hospitable. When I arrived at their farms with deliveries from Chelford, they would always say, 'Come on in lad and have a cup of tea.' I remember one particularly gruelling journey when the farmer insisted on giving me some whisky to warm me up. I'm not really a drinking man, but I didn't refuse.

The Wasted View

Many farmers don't have the time to appreciate the beautiful environment in which they live. On one delivery at a Derbyshire farm, I was having a cup of tea with the farmer when I noticed that the living room had a large window giving a panoramic view over a lovely valley with a reservoir in the distance.

'You have a wonderful view,' I said.

'Yes,' said the farmer, 'I suppose we do, but we never look at it.'

Delivering goods bought at Chelford to outlying farms could be a hair-raising business. I remember one journey in about 1956 to deliver some bales of straw that had been bought at Chelford by a farmer (whose name I didn't know at that point) out beyond Macclesfield in the direction of Buxton. There were no cabs on tractors in those days. Because the wind came from the west, journeys out eastwards beyond Chelford weren't too bad, as the load sheltered you from the elements. On the first part of the journey – the bit on the Cheshire plain – conditions were bearable. The snow had melted and the roads were clear of ice. But, as I got near to my destination in Rainow, there was hard-packed snow and drifts everywhere. Fog had also descended. I was driving a Ferguson T20 pulling an old ex-railway lorry. This would have been safe enough near to home where I knew the roads, but it was not equal to the conditions prevailing in that area.

The buyer had given me instructions on how to get to his farm – Wicken Ford – but I could hardly see and had to pull into a layby near a pub called The Setter Dog to look for the track. When I eventually found it, I realised that it disappeared down into a valley. Caution came over me and I decided that it would be foolish to attempt a descent in those treacherous conditions. I returned to my load and proceeded to throw the bales over the fence in the hope that the field alongside the layby was part of Wicken Ford Farm. The journey home was much colder than it had been coming as there was no load this time to shelter me from the wind. All the time, the temperature was dropping and the showers which had turned to snow were driving straight into my face. When I got back, I rang Chelford Market to confess what I had done. Thankfully, I still received their cheque promptly, so I realised that the bales must have landed in the right field!

Some time later, I was back at Chelford selling straw at an auction. Bidding is a quiet art involving a wink or a turn of the thumb. If you wanted to buy and were standing behind the auctioneer, you could actually just give him a prod in the back. After the first prod, the auctioneer would turn round to check who was bidding. Your ensuing prods would go unnoticed by the rest of the crowd, to the extent that that the other bidders might not even realise that you were taking part. Some buyers, on the other hand, were very up front in their bidding, raising their hand so as not to be missed. I was aware of one gentleman who placed his bids in this way. His name was Charlie Goodwin and he was obviously a hill farmer because he always came suitably dressed for the bleak conditions that prevailed in his area in a large ex-army greatcoat. It always amused me to see that to keep his legs warm, he wrapped them in plastic fertilizer sacks. Charlie always carefully contemplated what he wanted to buy whilst taking his lunch break. He carried a strong brown paper bag containing his sandwiches and munched away as he watched the loads being sold. As his bid was registered, the auctioneer would inevitably exclaim 'One for the Butty!' On this particular occasion, I had just the kind of straw that Charlie needed and the price was right. He won the bidding and I asked him where he wanted the straw to be delivered. I couldn't believe it when I found out that once again I was destined for Wicken Ford Farm.

On this second occasion, the conditions were just the same as the first time. The track down to the farm was on hard-packed snow and ice and was very slippery. The rumour going round the market at that time was that a trailer on a similar journey had tipped over. But, this time, I was not deterred; I had moved much heavier loads of up to eight tonnes in my time and this load of straw was only three tonnes, so I was confident I was safe. The track was flat for most of the way but then descended steeply to the farm in the valley between two stone walls. The driveway to the farm (having been cut out of the hillside) was just wide enough for the load. I took it with caution, applying the brakes gently to keep the speed slow. When I arrived, Charlie looked rather surprised that I had managed to drive all the way down into the yard. He would, he said, have expected me to unload higher up. I told him about my previous experience a few years earlier and he remembered finding the bales and reckoned that I had made the right decision that day.

Charlie and I unloaded the straw in a stone building. A motor wagon was unloading at the same time. Just before we lifted the last two bales off my trailer, a number of cows from an adjoining field came for an inspection. As the driveway was filled by my vehicle, they were able to climb from the field over the wall and onto the back of the trailer – something they couldn't normally do as the walls were 6ft high. After removing the cows and having a cup of tea, I was ready for home, but it wasn't to be that easy. The tractor tyres spun on the hard-packed snow. After I had made two or three attempts at backing up and taking a run at the hill, Charlie appeared on the scene with the fire shovel loaded with cinders out of the fireplace. Scattering these did the trick and I thought that I was at last on my way home. On nearing the main road, however, I encountered another problem. The road was on a slight incline and the motor wagon which had left before me was stuck. The men driving it had been waiting for me. I dropped my trailer and went back and towed them out. All things considered, it had been quite an exhausting day.

Some of the buyers at Chelford would try to buy directly from the farmers, especially if the prices on the day were high. Occasionally, they would come round to Yew Tree Farm to do a deal. One buyer approached me in the market about buying direct. He said that he had a small farm yard and wanted to buy a smaller amount of straw than I was selling that day. After I got home from the market that evening, he rang and asked if I could deliver the straw to his address. I was rather wary about doing this as he had mentioned that his farm was rather unapproachable. I asked him whether the farm track was worse than the one to Wicken Ford Farm. He said that it was about the same but that there was the added excitement of a ford to drive through. I wasn't worried about that as the stream had a solid bottom. I also reckoned that the weather was quite mild as spring was about to arrive, so I decided to chance it.

A few days later I made my way along the Congleton to Buxton road (known locally as 'Dumbers' because of its undulating pattern). Following the farmer's instructions, I reached a particular field where I had to get down from the cab to open the gate. It was only then that I realised what I had let myself in for. Just through the gate, the drive turned left and descended very sharply into a valley. I could see the farmstead nestled into a hillside at the opposite side of a stream. I got back into the tractor and turned into the field. The descent was so steep, I immediately lost sight of the drive. All I could see was the farm on the other side of the valley about a quarter of a mile away. I had to look in the small windows on either side of the tractor bonnet and watch the front wheels to keep them on the turning drive. After the steep descent, fording the stream was no problem. The yard was very small and I could see why the farmer had wanted a smaller load. Yet again I had survived a delivery from Chelford to an outlying farm.

Cattle: Beef and Dairy

The cattle dealers at Chelford are all different characters but they are all very shrewd. Some are local farmers who buy calves, rear them and sell them as stores to be fattened by someone else, and some market the animals at the slaughter stage. Most of the calf buyers are dealers who come from other parts of the country and buy to order for rearers who live in their area. Many of these men have a regular position in the cattle ring where they sit or stand. Things usually proceed in a sedate manner with the auctioneer in control and 100 calves or more probably go through the ring in an hour.

Anybody watching would probably be mystified about who was buying as (because the auctioneer or the clerks usually know the buyers) their names tend not to be announced. Only new buyers are asked their name or – more recently – their computer number. You can, however, usually establish who the buyer is by looking around the ring to see who is writing things down: the buyers usually record the sale numbers of the animals. Sometimes, after a sale, the seller will go in the box with the auctioneer and give the drover some 'luck' money as the animal is handed to the buyer.

A Belgian Blue Friesian bull calf being sold at Chelford, July 2007. The vendor is holding up a pound coin for luck. The auctioneer is Roy Waller. The proceedings are watched by the vendor's father, Alan, in the deerstalker hat.

The Drunken Cattle Dealer

Before the drink driving laws came in, cattle dealers used to be well-fuelled with alcohol. There used to be a cattle-dealing auction at the Lion pub in Warrington. This was in the days of the horse and trap and before traffic lights. One farmer, Bill Rowbotham, would never be sober. Before the end of the sale, he would be loaded into the trap by his friends and sent on his way down Bridge Street in the direction of the river. The policeman on point duty at Bridge Foot would then point the horse in the right direction for home.

I once spoke to a local policeman about a local cattle dealer who loved his beer. He said that this chap caused the police more trouble than the rest of the parish put together. When he was sober there was not a more sane person, but when he was 'with the boys', his whole personality changed. His language was not repeatable and some of the innuendos – especially when the ladies were present – were embarrassing. One afternoon, this fellow was enjoying a drinking session in a local club when the police came in and asked him to move his car as he was causing an obstruction. He gave the keys to a young companion. On getting into the car, the young fellow felt a wet sensation behind his ears. He turned round and was amazed to see three sheep that had been bought that morning in Carlisle Market!

The Cattle Dealers' Scissors

Cattle dealers used to carry a pair of scissors, usually in the top pocket of their jackets. With these, they would cut their initials into the cattle's hair to show which animals they had bought. In a bar one evening, a number of cattle dealers from Chelford were socialising when they noticed a man with a very large handlebar moustache. This became a challenge. It's hard to say which one of them actually sneaked up behind the man, but, with a quick snip of the scissors, the moustache was soon gone.

Cattle dealers in some people's eyes are akin to Ali Baba and the forty thieves, but quite often they are useful in finding a solution to an immediate problem. Father once had a bull of about five to six years old that he wanted to sell at Chelford. Between 1959 and 1964 there was a slump in the price of bulls. This was partly because artificial insemination had been introduced at that time by the Milk Marketing Board and it was no longer necessary for every farm to keep one. In addition, bull beef didn't appeal to the tastebuds of the British public. Ike Powell – one of the cattle dealers at Chelford – had his own solution to this: he sold British bull meat to the American occupational forces in Europe.

Ike knew a lot about bulls and when Father got to Chelford, he took note of our bull and evidently wanted to buy it. Another dealer was a neighbour of ours and indicated that he would help Father get a good price for the bull, despite the current economic situation. It's the custom that if the seller is proud of their animal, they will go onto the rostrum with the auctioneer and tell everybody what a wonderful beast they have the chance of buying. Father did this, but his speech alone would not have done the trick. The auctioneer got into his stride and soon had his first bid – from Ike Powell. The bidding continued to move at a fast pace as a result of our neighbour using his walking stick and prodding the auctioneer every so often in the back. Ike was forced to raise his price to win the bid. Much to Father's satisfaction, he got a very good price for the bull and came home like a dog with two tails.

The Cheshire Climate

The climate in Cheshire is not very good for haymaking but the county is one of the best areas for growing grass in the British Isles with a mild climate and an abundance of rain. It doesn't suffer badly even when the rest of the country is experiencing drought conditions. At the Royal Agricultural Show in Warwickshire, Jack Scott, one of the television weather presenters, once told me that he couldn't predict anything with certainty about the weather in Cheshire because of our geographical location next to Liverpool Bay. This apparently acts as a thermal basin with the consequence that heavy showers frequently come through the 'Cheshire Gap' between the Welsh Hills and the Pennines.

Because of its great grass-growing potential, Cheshire is one of the best milk-producing areas in the British Isles. As you would expect, Chelford Market has a section especially for the sale of cows for producing milk. The dealers in the dairy section, like the calf buyers, have their regular places around the ring. To an outsider, it must be difficult to appreciate the need for cattle to move about the ring, but this is necessary to enable buyers and sellers to establish a price. Private deals are done in the dairy section much as they are in every other part of Chelford Market.

There are a few farmers who rear heifer claves. They get them in calf and then sell them when they are near to calving or newly calved, into the dairy section. Uncle Frank was one of these. He once went to pick one up with my friend Prickle. When they returned to Old Farm and opened the doors of the wagon, another animal that they were transporting ran out in a very frightened state and escaped into the surrounding countryside! It took hours for them to retrieve it.

Pigs, Sheep and Poultry

Chelford Market also had thriving pig and sheep sections. It even sold rabbits, gerbils and hamsters – but it was the poultry section that was of most interest to the general public. Every type of bird was to be found there including all the traditional breeds of hens, bantams and ducks, as well as exotic or rare breeds such as pigeons, tumbler doves, and even sporting birds such as quail. I have even seen peacocks sold there. During the breeding season there are hatching eggs for sale, all different sizes from ostrich eggs down to quail eggs. Anyone who is producing eggs in a small way can go along and buy point-of-lay pullets, keep them for a year or two for the eggs, and return with the birds at the end of their laying life to sell them as 'boiling fowl.'

An RSPCA officer would be keeping an eye on things in this part of the market. He was a very well-respected member of the local community. Sometimes, buyers would take a fancy to the birds but would not think about how they were to get them home. The officer then had to offer the best advice to the buyer with the interest of the bird or the animal to the fore.

Valuations

The auctioneers and staff at Chelford Market were well known over a large area. This was partly because they used to come out of the market and organise farm sales when a farmer was retiring. Their valuation was crucial because it determined the pension that a farmer or his wife might get. Prices were determined by two things: first by the well-being of the cattle and the state of the machinery on the day of the sale (these were things the retiring farmer could control); and secondly by the state of agriculture in the general economy (this he had no control over). If a retiring farmer was handing the business over to his son, there would be no farm sale, but, nevertheless, a valuation was sometimes useful for tax purposes and for the interest of other members of the family.

In the early 1950s, Chelford Market was expanding and a new auctioneer was taken on. His name was Harold Shillaker. The first time I met him was when he came to do a valuation at Yew Tree Farm in about 1960 when Father handed it over to me. Everything connected to the farm was valued. Cows, poultry, horses etc were classed as 'livestock': tractors and implements were classed as 'deadstock'. A valuation was also done of crops in the ground like autumn-sown crops. Unexhausted manures were taken into account too, as were fixtures, like hen houses, which were classed as temporary buildings and would not be included in the potential rent of the farm. When Father took Mr Shillaker round for his valuation, Willy Moore and I were mowing the hay and they came into the field to value the tractor and the old mowing machine which Willy was operating. On seeing Willy, Mr Shillaker enquired whether he too was a fixture. This was very apt as Willy had worked at Yew Tree Farm for twenty-seven years.

'The Junk Sale'

One department of Chelford that has developed a great deal over the years has been the one offering second-hand machinery – this is affectionately known as the 'Junk Sale.' It's actually a chance for farmers to change their method of farming by putting their machinery up for sale. There is everything here from garden shears to large hedge cutters, from a small lawn mower to the most sophisticated silage machinery. If somebody is selling a machine because they think that it is coming to the end of its useful life, they will probably get a better price for it at Chelford than in trade against a new machine. And of course, it's better to sell it at Chelford than to have it rusting at the back of the farm complex with nettles growing up around it – waiting to be cannibalised for scrap.

Other Aspects of the Market

In recent years, Chelford has diversified into all sorts of other goods. There are now twice-weekly sales of vegetables, bedding plants, flowers, shrubs and trees. Eggs are also sold in large quantities. This has brought shopkeepers into the market – people who would never in the past have visited Chelford. It also brings together people with farm shops who, if they have a surplus of their own products can sell it, or if they are short of some items, can stock up. Visiting Chelford keeps people in touch with market trends. It also gives opportunists a chance to buy something cheap from an overstocked market and then make a killing out of it.

During the school holidays a lot of schoolchildren visit the market with their parents who are there on business. On Bank Holidays, the market is alive with families from all walks of life. Sometimes a teacher will bring her children on an educational visit. On one such visit, I believe, the teacher assembled the class on the seats in the calf ring. It wasn't long before one of the cattle buyers, a character called Charlie Bell from Aberdeen, had stopped the sale of the calves and was conducting the children in singing in a choir. I am sure the children never forgot their day at Chelford.

Perhaps the highlight of Chelford Market for me was when Granada Television once sent a camera crew and reporter to make a programme for their country special, *Down to Earth*, which was shown on a Sunday afternoon. The crew were seen in most areas of the market interviewing likely characters. One day a Welsh buyer was loading up his lorry and trailer. The reporter saw this as an opportunity for an interview but failed to realise that Mr Davies – the buyer – wasn't a television personality. He hadn't the time or the inclination to speak, so he replied to the questions in Welsh. The interview was soon over! The crew came down off the loads looking very despondent and were still seeking some information on what was happening. As I was hanging about waiting to unload onto Mr Davies's trailer, I volunteered to string a few words together about the reasons why farmers came to Chelford – to sell their stock or produce, to buy the same, to visit the stalls on the market site for items such as Wellington boots and working clothes, to make private deals or simply to have a drink in the Dixon Arms. It seemed to go down well enough. This was my one and only experience of dealing with the media and I must say that I rather enjoyed it.

Chelford Market is different things to different people – to some it is serious business, to others a meeting place where old acquaintances are renewed. To some it is a zoo, and to some a place to eat whilst the 'missus' goes shopping. That vicar never spoke a truer word, however, than when he said that – to farmers – Chelford is the centre of the universe.

Local cattle dealer Ike Powell appraising a bull, 1960s.

EIGHT

The 1950s – Changes On and Around the Farm

In the late 1950s and early 1960s, a number of important changes occurred in the local area: familiar buildings were taken over for new purposes, the M6 motorway was built just a stone's throw from our land, and farming became more sophisticated and more mechanised. All these changes had an effect on our daily lives and on the countryside around us.

The Transformation of Meadowlands

In 1956, Meadowlands, where the Dunkerley family had once lived, was sold to British Gas and was developed into a training college for the staff of their North-West Division. A lot of people wondered what the training was all about. Gas plumbers obviously had to have an apprenticeship before qualifying but it looked as though what was taught at the college was nothing to do with that. In fact, it seemed as if the only thing the students were being taught there was how to present themselves to the housewife! All this was even more puzzling when you took into consideration the fact that most gas cookers at that time were sold through gas showrooms. Was there really any need for super gas salesmen?

The local MP Sir William Bromley Davenport was asking similar questions about the college in the House of Commons. His interest was apparently causing an embarrassment and he was invited by the college to pay a visit. Mere College, as it was then known, had five-star cuisine with standards set by the housekeeper, Marjorie Carney. Sir Walter enjoyed a superb meal, drinks and conversation with the lecturers who were experts in their field. It seemed that he was so impressed by the hospitality that his reservations about the place disappeared overnight. We never heard another peep out of him!

Mother's sister, Aunty Gerty, had joined the staff of Mere College as a secretary. This was strange for Mother, who had obviously worked there as a girl as the Dunkerley's nanny. Auntie Gerty enjoyed her job: she had a good appetite (sometimes she was known as 'The Dustbin') and she probably made the most of her midday meal. The college had a wonderful garden which, although it was tended by three different gardeners, was immaculate. The gardeners were Ben Passant, who lived in the lodge and had been a chauffeur gardener all his life (he was getting on a bit and had lost the spring in his step), Bill Kerfoot, who was an ex farm-worker who had had an accident with a bull (which had left him with a limp), and Percy Shakeshaft, (who had had polio in his younger days). They were good gardeners, but all immobile to some degree!

Aunty Gerty Ties the Knot

Aunty Gerty was thought to be rather choosey when she was young but she eventually married a widower, Dennis Cook, who already had a grown-up family. It was a quiet wedding with her brother, Uncle Frank, as best man, and sister Bertha as matron of honour. As they signed the register, Uncle Frank, who never missed an opportunity for dry humour, couldn't help remarking, 'Well Dennis, tha's got to the point of no return now!'

The Building of the M6

There are days in your life that you will never forget – days that mark a milestone for you and sometimes for the whole area in which you live. One afternoon in 1963 we were doing some draining in one of the fields at Yew Tree Farm with the tractor-mounted excavator. It was a very still, cold day and we were completely in a world of our own surrounded by a thick fog. We could just about make out the trench we were digging but we couldn't see the outline of the field hedges, let alone the trees in them. In fact, we had not seen the sky or the sun all day and all we could hear was the noise of the tractor as it worked the excavator.

The light was failing and when I realised that I couldn't even see the bubbles on the spirit level to make sure that we 'had fall' on the drain, I knew that it was time to go back to the farm and milk the cows. David, our farm worker, stopped the tractor. We expected total silence on a cold, still day like that. How wrong we were! It appeared that something in a nearby field was making a loud roaring noise. The strange thing was that the noise was constant, it didn't vary at all in pitch or tone. We were puzzled: it couldn't be anyone working a machine on a nearby farm. It was a noise we had never heard before. It was only as we walked back to Yew Tree that we realised that the M6 motorway was being opened that afternoon.

The building of the M6 and other motorways was surely the biggest intrusion into the countryside since the canals in the eighteenth century and the railways in the nineteenth century. In North Cheshire, the M6 was broadly welcomed because the existing roads (including the A50, which ran directly past the farm) were not able to cope with the increasing amount of freight being carried by road vehicles. Most people who lived in the countryside were probably too busy to complain about the building of the M6, but there were those who did oppose it. One of these was a man who had bought a farm as a country residence. He had to have a large earth mound constructed between his house and the motorway to block out the noise. The next-door farm, by contrast, was right against the hard shoulder and the noise must have been horrendous.

There was other disruption too. The firm that built the M6 locally was called Tarmac. They bought out numerous quarries in Derbyshire so that they had all the sand and gravel they needed to build the carriageway. All this had to be transported on the ordinary roads. Tarmac also erected a mixing plant in the local area to make concrete for the bridges. At roughly the same time that the motorway was being built, electricity pylons were erected and fuel and gas pipes were laid across land in the area. None of this upheaval brought much benefit to the immediate locality. The pylons and pipes were part of a national network and the local people were not particularly interested at the time. In more recent years there has been some concern about the risk to health potentially caused by static electricity from the high-tension cables in the neighbourhood which carry up to 275,000 volts. The high proportion of local deaths from cancer has been attributed to these overhead wires, but nothing has ever been proved.

The Green Revolution

In 1946, the Director General of the United Nations Food and Agriculture Organization, Sir John Boyd Orr, had announced that the world was in danger of suffering a catastrophic famine within twenty years. To ensure that this didn't happen, over the next decade and beyond, farmers were encouraged to produce more food to feed the nation and to help the balance of payments. Plant breeders, fertilizer manufacturers and agricultural engineers set about giving farmers the tools to do the job.

If the land were to yield more, soil fertility had to be improved. At Yew Tree Farm, we started to use artificial fertilizers but these needed to be countered with lime to maintain the correct PH or acidity level. Traditionally, the lime used in Cheshire came from Derbyshire and, after the introduction of artificial fertilizers, it was used in much larger quantities. There was an opportunity here for some quick-thinking agricultural type to make a lot of money.

Adam Lythgoe was the very fellow. Born on a small farm near Leigh, Warrington, he became one of the great agricultural entrepreneurs of his time. Not only did he operate locally, but he also expanded over a wide area of the British Isles, ably assisted by his sons: Adam Junior, Fred and Joe. Adam Lythgoe began by selling manure, but he made his money by securing the contract to remove a waste product from the locally-based chemical company ICI. After burnt lime had been used in their chemical-making process, there was a product left over called 'waste lime.' This had a neutralizing effect on acid soils and Adam Lythgoe saw its potential. With the increased use of artificial fertilizers and the amount of sulphur coming out of the atmosphere from industry, he correctly anticipated that there would be an increasing demand from farmers for lime.

One of the secrets of the Lythgoe's success, in my opinion, was that they used housewives to do their selling. The ladies worked from their own homes and used their own phones. One, named Betty, had a wonderful sales patter. She knew just when to phone, after the working day was over and once you had had your tea. This was the time when farmers did their bookkeeping. Sometimes it was a welcome relief at these times to get a phone call from a lady with a pleasant voice.

A calf at Yew Tree Farm.

Keeping the Lingo

Despite their fortune, the enterprising Lythgoes, to their credit, kept their Lancashire roots and accent. This was a great asset to them when they were dealing with farmers. There is nothing more off-putting to a farmer in a salesperson than an Oxford accent – especially if you are a bit dubious about purchasing the item in the first place!

Adam Lythgoe could sell anything. I remember once being involved in a Young Farmers' Debate. We would often pontificate about imaginary situations. I suggested that you could grow kale to feed cattle and that, if you had surplus, you could sell it. The opposition were scornful, saying that you would never find a buyer for kale. I replied with just the two words, 'Adam Lythgoe'. It probably didn't get me any points with the judges, but it certainly raised laughter from the audience.

The Lythgoes seemed to be very good organisers: their sales people were paid on commission, and the men who carted and spread the lime were all self-employed. All this was before mass privatisation at a time when most of the other big firms and manufacturers were using nationalised transport. Lythgoe's workers mostly came from an agricultural background and many later became very successful haulage contractors in their own right.

One Over the Eight

I once went to Liverpool to pick up some fertilizer from Lythgoes. I assumed that they would be well-organised and that the scams that I had heard about which apparently often happened on the dockside would be controlled. I was wrong. I had been told that I would drive over a weighbridge which would check the tare weight of my vehicle. The first thing that happened was that a man approached me selling gentlemen's toiletries! He was actually the ganger (in charge of both the men in the ships' holds loading the slings and of the men who were helping each driver load his vehicle on the dockside). Later he came to talk to me again. He had realised that I was a farmer and suggested a cheap price for an extra tonne of fertilizer. I explained that my trailer's load was eight tonnes and I couldn't legally take any more. As I drove home, I sensed the difference between the innocent countryside and the streetwise city. I was getting educated. No self-respecting docker would have been worried about one over the eight!

Joe Eckhart: Haulage Contractor

One of the haulage contractors who started out working for Adam Lythgoe was Joe Eckart. He had been in the German Navy in the U-Boats. Although he had settled in this country after the war, he was proud of his naval achievements. Joe liked farmers. Once after taking a load to his farm at The Moss, Wilmslow, I fell into conversation with him and he told me he used to go to America for reunions with other survivors from the war. He also went back to Germany on a regular basis and would bring a large supply of Rhineland wine back with him. I'm sure that he relished working for Lythgoes and was proud to have their large signs on his wagons, one placed high up behind the cab, and the other at the rear.

The turnover of staff working for Joe was fairly high. He was a hard task master and expected everyone to work at the same high rate as himself. Most of the work handling lime and other products would be what we call 'fork and shovel' labour. One of Joe's employees once told me that they went to a pharmaceutical centre which kept animals. Their task was to move a huge amount of manure manually. Never afraid to get his hands dirty, Joe forked manure onto the elevator and his two men loaded it onto the wagon. They then swapped roles and Joe loaded the wagon whilst the men loaded it onto the elevator. In both cases, Joe urged the other two on to greater and greater effort, until they could almost bear it no longer.

A friend of mine who worked for Joe for a short period told me that he would repair his wagons all through the night, making sure that they were back at base and ready for work in the morning. My friend took one of Joe's wagons to Minera Quarry in Wales to pick up magnesium limestone. It was a hair-raising journey as the wagon had no brakes. On arriving at the quarry, the man phoned Joe to report this. Joe just told him to get the wagon loaded stating that, 'if the wagon has no brakes, you drive accordingly!'

I didn't go to Joe's funeral, but I am told that it was very well attended. He had a wreath in the shape of a U-Boat – the main part in white flowers with the identification number in red!

Silage Making

During the 1950s, there were some very wet summers, which resulted in very poor hay, and sometimes even crop loss. You had to feed the cows on something and the answer was silage. To make silage you had to use molasses. Sometimes we couldn't resist dipping our finger in the tin and having a taste. The idea was to mix the molasses with water and spread it on each layer of grass with a watering can that had had the rose removed and a spoon tied on the end. This gave a good even spread of what was rather a thick liquid.

A Sticky Problem

A friend of mine didn't use a watering can when pouring molasses on the silage but simply threw bucketfuls of the stuff on the grass. I suggested that the process could be a bit messy and he laughed and said that it did occasionally get up his trouser leg making the hairs on his legs sticky. Apparently, when he got into bed at night his wife sometimes complained that their legs were sticking together!

Silage-making wasn't very popular with some farmers' wives because of the smell that it caused around the farmyard, and in the house, if it got onto your clothes. Once you had spread the liquid, you had to try not to walk on the grass until a new layer of grass had been put on top. It was also advisable to wear Wellingtons as the molasses could be cleaned off these easily. One night, my friend Bob and I had planned to go to Manchester to see the show *South Pacific*. Before we left, it was my job to give the cows a big forkful of silage after the afternoon's milking. That evening, I had actually asked Willie Moore to feed the cows so that I could get cleaned up before going to the theatre, but because I was ready early, I decided, in the end, to do it myself. Rather stupidly, I didn't think to get changed again.

Bob appeared and we went off to Manchester. In the interval we went to buy an ice cream and Bob's nose started to twitch. He asked me if I had been feeding the cows earlier. I had to admit that I had, but I was surprised that he could smell the silage on me as I could have sworn that it hadn't touched my clothes. This was the heyday of the musicals and there was a saying that 'when the music stops, the melody lingers on'. The same can be said of the smell of silage! I will always remember one of the songs in *South Pacific* that night. It was called, 'I'm going to wash that man right out of my hair'. I realised that the same can't be said of silage. If you have been near it, the smell hangs about!

Combine Harvesters

The biggest change to farming in the 1950s, of course, was the mechanisation of harvesting. The days of the threshing machine were numbered and combine harvesters were becoming more popular. It was not only the method of harvesting the crop that was changing, but also the way the grain was handled – a change from sacks to bulk. Some combines had both hooks on which to hang sacks and a grain tank for bulk handling.

Combine harvesters were advertised in the farming press and were manufactured by The International Harvester Company – which was a worldwide business. In 1961, I wrote off for a specification and a price list and, a while afterwards, a cheerful character called to see me unannounced. His name was Giles Kitchen and he was the rep from a firm called Agricultural Machinery from Nantwich. This company was well-established in Cheshire and, at that time, the nobility of the farming community would have said that if you didn't know Giles Kitchen, your education wasn't complete. Giles had done his research and evidently knew enough about me to know that I would pay up. Strangely enough, I didn't know Giles. In fact, at that point, I had never even heard of him.

Giles told me that there was a new combine on the market that had been built and tested in France. I agreed to try it and soon it was delivered and commissioned for work. I wasn't quite ready to use it yet, however. One day, before the harvest was ready, Giles appeared in the potato field. His first mistake was to say, 'Hello Grandad,' to Willie Moore, which didn't put Willie in a very good mood. Giles then suggested that we should try the combine out. I didn't feel that the crop was ripe enough, but Giles insisted.

It appeared that there were combines in the South of France that were not performing properly. Giles had a man with him from that area and they wanted to see how my machine performed. The trial was a complete failure. The Frenchman was very upset about the performance of the machine and blamed the big English crop. In fact, he got very excited about the whole episode and started flinging his hands about and making a lot of gestures. Giles reckoned that if you had tied his arms behind his back he would have been speechless. That night, Giles came round with a proposition. Either they gave me my money back, or, for some more money, they would sell me a Claas combine which he could guarantee would work.

The Claas combine was eventually delivered. The field of oats was ready: the weather was fine. Giles said that he would tutor me in how to use the machine. In fact, he just drove around the field once. When he got back to the gate, it transpired that he had run out of cigarettes and I was dispatched to get some more – they were an essential part of his personality. When I got back, I realised my lesson was over. Giles dismounted, said, 'You'll be all right,' and gave me the firm's telephone number in case I needed it. With that, he disappeared out of the field. That was my introduction to combining. Willie and I successfully finished the harvest with the new combine and even did some combining for other farmers with it.

Corncrakes

You can't mechanise farming and expect the countryside to stay exactly the same. The modern way of cutting grass with mowing machines brought about the virtual extinction of a bird known as the corncrake. Corncrakes were a ground-nesting bird and, unfortunately, they nested at the same time that the hay was ready for cutting. The hen bird was very reluctant to move off the nest and this meant that the fast-moving mowing machine often chopped her head off. Father told me that over the years, the numbers of these birds was consistently falling as the number of mowing machines in the countryside rose. In the old days, the slower moving man with a scythe gave the nesting bird more time, and more importantly, probably saw the bird and deliberately mowed around the nest in the hope that the eggs would soon hatch out and the brood could then be moved to the safety of the hedge. Protecting the corncrakes was one of the reasons why Father continued using the scythe.

A Mowing Competition

There was once a wager made between a group of men about who could mow the largest area with a scythe. The bet was made in a pub. One man was far less skilled than the others and knew that he was bound to lose, so he decided to do something about it. He put a laxative in the glass of the man that he thought might win the competition. Next day, the better mower was soon into his stride. Then, of course, the laxative started to take its effect. He had to make many trips out of the field, soon surrendered the lead and looked like losing. Like all the men who mowed with a scythe, though, this man was a man of great stamina and endurance. He didn't give up but continued to mow between the interruptions and finally returned to the field minus his trousers. He eventually won the contest despite his opponent's skulduggery.

In fact, I only heard a corncrake once when Father pointed out a noise in the still evening air. It was the first time he had heard it in years. It wasn't a pleasing sound actually but a shrill, grating noise and I couldn't really understand why Father was sad it had gone. The corncrake survived on the small farms of Western Ireland and the crofts of Scotland. Here, there were small fields and the grass continued to be cut with a scythe.

Willie Moore Retires

One of the saddest changes that occurred on the farm in the 1960s was that Willie Moore – the farm hand who had worked for us for twenty-seven years – announced one day in 1962 that he was going to leave us. He was going to try to get a job with the council in Irlam, near Warrington, where his wife's family lived. We had just had a new milking machine installed in the new shippon and Willie understood the workings of these things better than anyone. We would really miss his expertise, but his retirement meant much more than that. He had been a huge influence on my life having been with us from before I went to school until quite a while after I was married.

As well as contributing invaluable work on the farm, Willie had been a vital source of local information. He had lived latterly at Hoo Green (a local area which consisted of about ten cottages and twelve council houses) and he had always helped his friends and neighbours. In particular, he had been a regular visitor to Albi Percival at Holly House Farm on his way home from work, and had helped him with his farm chores when he was too ill to do them. Now he wouldn't be doing that anymore. When Willie left it was the end of an era for many of us. Even now, I wonder whether the fact that things had changed so much on the farm during the 1950s contributed to Willie's decision to move on.

NINE

Crops and Animals

Life on a farm is always varied. At Yew Tree, we were busy all year round growing potatoes, wheat, barley and oats. We also kept chickens and cattle and – at one point – were even involved with the breeding of rabbits. Each line of business brought us into contact with its own array of country characters and provided us with some very funny stories.

Potatoes

We were what is known in farming circles as 'early potato growers.' This is a business that has its own kind of risks. Among early potato growers, there is a strong fear of frost. Uncle Frank used to talk about Jack Frost as if he were a character like Father Christmas who came sweeping down the A50 road. Instead of giving out presents, he froze the crops. There are certain low-lying areas, especially mossy ground – like some areas of North Cheshire – that are always susceptible to Jack. In higher areas, soft fruits are at risk. No farmer with any experience would plant potatoes before the frost risk had expired. 1 April is the generally agreed date at which potatoes should be planted, but over the years, some of us have planted them as early as St Patrick's Day (17 March). I remember one special year, Father had bought ten bags of the new variety – Ulster Chieftain. We took a risk and planted them in mid-March near to the A50 road. The Percivals, our neighbours down the road at Holly House Farm, had done the same. That year Jack Frost came at the end of May and he was severe. All the potatoes that had surfaced on farms nearby were, as Uncle Frank put it, completely 'decimated.' That time we were lucky. For some unknown reason, our crop and the Percival's survived. Uncle Frank suggested that Jack Frost had come along the A50 very fast, and our few potatoes were 'not worth pulling up for.'

The Potato Exchange

The price of local new potatoes was set at the Potato Exchange held in the Appleton Thorn pub three days a week. Here, many local farmers and potato merchants got together armed with the day's market prices and possible future trends. On the basis of this information, they gave a recommended price. The meeting at the Potato Exchange was a sociable occasion. Robin Jones – our friendly NFU Secretary – loved attending, as it put him in touch with a lot of farmers, and he certainly relished his visit to the pub three times a week.

Our own potato sales at the farm gate increased a lot over the years. Kathleen was mainly responsible for this but Father also got involved. People who called to buy potatoes were

Spinning out early potatoes on a Massey Fergusson 35. Early potatoes at Yew Tree Farm are grown in the part of this field that borders the A50 road. It is said that this land is a gravel deposit from the last Ice Age.

always impressed by Father's great age. By 1972, although he was in his mid eighties and had been working on the farm since the age of eleven, he still wanted to be actively involved.

Selling potatoes brought us into contact with people from all over the country as well as with the locals. Some were regulars. These included a man named Frank whom we called 'the praitee man' who worked for an animal feed merchants and general haulage business. His run was from the cement works at Cauldon Low in Staffordshire to the Liverpool/South Lancashire area. He took corn in one direction and copper ingots from Prescot in the other. Another regular was the man who drove the Quantock Jam Wagon. He came from Somerset loaded up with bulk jam destined for Hartley's biscuit factory in Liverpool.

One potato buyer who only called at the farm once has stayed in my memory. He was a man in a mini van with a strong Irish accent. He asked, 'You have potatoes – the new ones I presume?' I replied that we had.
'Well, it's not the new ones I want – it's the old ones. Would you be having any of them?' I explained that we had as we kept some for purchase by Mere College across the road. We could let him have a bag if he called again as we had none sorted out right then. The man said that he wouldn't be coming this way again and that if I didn't mind, he would help me sort them out. So we kneeled down in the potato hog together and started rubbing the sprits off the old potatoes. I remember we had a conversation about the registration of his van – the number had been painted on the rear doors with white paint. He had been warned that it was an offence not to have an illuminated number plate, but he had apparently told the police that it would have to be a constable with very poor eyesight who couldn't read his sign! After some chatting and sorting, the two of us managed to collect one bag of old potatoes. At this point, the man said, 'Do you think you could be letting me have a second bag?' I said I could and we carried on sorting the potatoes on our hands and knees: the conversation moved on to other aspects of his van. Just as we finished the man said, 'Do you think you could be letting me have another bag?' It was really my dinnertime and the meal would be spoiled, but we were having a laugh, so I agreed. Then the man said, 'Actually, I've been thinking. If you just

give me three bags of any potatoes, by the time I get round to eating them, I'm sure the new ones will have become old ones themselves!'

Poultry

A lot of farmers living along main roads keep hens so that they can sell the eggs to passing trade along with their potatoes. One lady used to call us the 'egg and chip' area. We used to buy a hundred day-old chickens every year and great preparations were made for their arrival. For one thing, we had to get the paraffin lamps working in order to keep the henhouse warm. We also had to make sure that the place was rat-proof – a day-old chicken was a delicacy to a rat. If the weather was suitable we kept the chickens on a free-range system and then shut them up at night to prevent the foxes getting in amongst them. In all, we had about 250 hens at any one time and the income from them supplemented what we got from potatoes. Until he had tried our eggs, Robin Jones, the NFU representative, used to say that there was no difference in the quality of eggs from hens kept in batteries, in deep litter or free-range. But after he had had our eggs once, he kept coming back for more. His wife insisted that these were the best eggs he had ever brought her.

One morning soon after getting some new chicks, I was awoken by the telephone in our bedroom. We had installed it as Mother and Father got older so that my sister Joyce could ring us if there was a problem. Joyce asked if I had forgotten to shut the hens up for the night as they seemed to be in a very frightened state and were making a terrible noise.

There was no time to think about clothes,: I just pulled on my Wellingtons and picked up the gun. I always wear a vest, but I have to admit that on this occasion, it was my summer version and it was a bit on the short side! I made my way down to the henhouses as quickly as possible. The fox had left, but I was greeted by a scene of awful destruction. They say that vixens will only take one hen, just enough to feed her cubs. If that is the case then this must have been a dog fox because he had left a trail of death and destruction behind him and had killed about thirty hens. I suppose the threat of foxes is one of the pitfalls of keeping free-range hens. As a farmer, you certainly feel vengeful after an event like this, not just because of the financial losses you have incurred, but also because of the unnecessary suffering that has been caused.

The Overweight Huntsman

I have never personally been involved in fox-hunting, but I can understand how it has come about. From my experience of shooting foxes, a large number get away wounded. By comparison, a killing by a hound must, in my opinion, be very quick, final and therefore less cruel. The only time I saw a foxhunt was before the M6 motorway was built. The huntsmen came down Dobb Lane next to the farm in all their finery.

As I watched, I noticed that the hunt was being followed by a group of early hunt protestors. They were in a quandary because one of the guests in the hunt was the radio, film and TV personality Jimmy Edwards. Jimmy was famous for being very large. From what the protestors were shouting, it became apparent that they were divided over which was the more cruel – the treatment of the fox or the weight of Jimmy Edwards on his poor horse!

By 1970, poultry breeding was becoming quite a science with local farmers crossbreeding to get hens with a better performance and farmers more rigorously recording the number of eggs laid. This was before the international companies came in with their own hybrid varieties. There was one farm locally which specialised in crossing Rhode Island Red hens with White

Leghorns. The resulting chickens grew into medium-sized hens which were prolific layers of good-sized eggs.

Uncle Frank had been using chickens from this local supplier with considerable success for a number of years. It came to his attention, however, that a new progressive breeder was operating locally using Brown Leghorn hens. As Uncle Frank's main source of income came from keeping laying hens, he (like a lot of other local farmers), thought he would be progressive and try some. Initially, the breed was very successful. After a few years, however, a problem arose when the pullets were coming into lay. There were a lot of fatalities from a condition known as 'round heart.' This was something inherent in the breeding of the Brown Leghorn and it had only just come to light.

There was another problem connected with the Brown Leghorn breed – the birds were 'flighty.' If you didn't give a knock on the henhouse door before opening it you would scare the living daylights out of them. If the hens were out in the field and somebody fired a gun or made some similar noise, they would probably end up in the next parish! After the problem with round heart, Uncle Frank decided to forget the Brown Leghorns and return to his previous supplier. He contacted the Brown Leghorn breeder, who wasn't in, but his wife said that they wouldn't really be concerned about the loss of a local order as they were now exporting the birds to Europe. In fact, she said, her husband was at the airport right then booking in a supply to send to France. Uncle Frank said wryly that he didn't think they needed to be taken to the airport, as he reckoned that they could fly there by themselves!

Hens and Balers

Laying hens don't always get it right as far as producing eggs go. They start off with small or 'pullet' eggs. Occasionally, the shell-making mechanism goes wrong and the egg is just enclosed in a sack called a 'soft-shelled egg'. Sometimes, there is a double yolked egg – where the hen has accidentally laid an egg about fifty percent longer than normal with two yolks in it.

This reminds me of something funny that once happened with our Massey Ferguson baler. The machine was probably one of the world's first pick-up balers. It had originally been used in North America and it was the only kind of baler in this country with needles on the side. To get through gateways, a mechanism had to be tripped to reduce the width of the machine. This resulted in a small bale being made. Sometimes the baler had a peculiar habit of missing tripping – a fact which resulted in a double-length bale.

On one particular occasion, the baler was doing its job under the supervision of our helper David. The first bale was soft as it had come into the bale chamber from the previous field. The second was just half a bale resulting from the needles being tripped. After that, the baler missed tripping which resulted in a double-length bale. The baler continued to progress around the field and, apart from the odd double-length bale, it was doing a good job. When asked how the Ferguson was performing, Uncle Frank thought for a moment and then said with his typical wry humour, 'Well, she set off with a soft-shelled one, then a pullet egg and the next a double-yoked!'

The Fear of Fowl Pest

There have always been diseases and infections in livestock. In the 1940s and 1950s, these usually developed quite slowly and farmers would suffer only small losses. The outbreak of Newcastle Disease or Fowl Pest in 1964-5 was different. The infection was carried quickly from farm to farm either by the wind or by wild birds like house sparrows. Many farmers in the area kept laying hens having been encouraged to do so by the government. Some farmers kept hens in battery cages, but they were also kept in old Army huts and lofts that were not being used for storage. Those hens not in battery cages were kept on deep litter – something that they could scratch in and in which they were safe from foxes.

You first realised that your hens had Fowl Pest when they stopped eating and drinking. The symptoms of Fowl Pest were like flu; the birds would be quiet apart from coughs and sneezes. There were still eggs in the pipeline but the numbers diminished until, after about a week, there were no eggs at all. This particular strain of Fowl Pest was not really a killer. The birds would take about eight weeks to get laying again, but would never reach their former egg-producing potential. My sister Joyce had about 750 laying hens in the shed near to the house in which she lived with Mother and Father and we also had about 250 hens that we kept on a traditional free-range basis. Strangely, although both lots of birds got the disease, they didn't get it at exactly the same time, even though they were in close proximity to each other. Another strange thing about Fowl Pest as it swept across the countryside was that it didn't seem to affect every farm. My friend J.P.'s farm, for instance, missed it entirely, but then again, I always said he was lucky!

In 1964, it was recommended that we vaccinate the birds individually with a 'dead' vaccine. This was a laborious job and very stressful for the birds. Uncle Frank kept a large number of laying birds, so, like Joyce, his income was seriously affected. We three devised a scheme to help each other. At both Old Farm and Yew Tree Farm, Uncle Frank and I caught the birds while Joyce administered the vaccine with a gun. We did this at night when the birds were perching, moving along with a flash light and giving each bird what Uncle Frank called 'a poke'.

Memories in the Hen Shed

Uncle Frank had been in the First World War but it was something he usually never talked about. He had no time for the Germans and sometimes, listening to him, it seemed as if he had even less time for the French. One night, as we were moving along the perches in the hen shed, poking, he told us about joining the Army and going to Catterick Camp. He reckoned that in his unit, there were men from all walks of life, every trade and profession you could think of. But, after ten weeks, he said, everybody was acting and thinking as one unit. I never worked out quite what, but something about those hen sheds at night had reminded him of his Army experiences.

We went on with this difficult vaccination process for a few years. It seemed to be a very time-consuming way of going about things, particularly as we knew that other countries were using a live vaccine which could be put into the hen's drinking water. Ken Whalley, the vet from Knutsford, said that the government veterinary officers had given British farmers the wrong advice. We should, he thought, have been using the live vaccine. Ken was frustrated. 'Why is it,' he said, 'that we drive on the left when the rest of the world drives on the right?'

In 1973, a new and more damaging strain of Fowl Pest affected Cheshire farms. This strain seemed to be totally immune to the vaccines being used and was devastating the country. The losses endured by farmers this time were very high: a large percentage of the birds that contracted the disease died, and those that recovered seemed very listless and never laid many eggs again. In fact, the effects of this epidemic meant that my sister, Joyce, stopped keeping hens. In addition, the disease had a terrible effect on wild birds. The sparrow population seemed decimated afterwards, perhaps because their main source of food was in the infected hen houses.

At a meeting of the local branch of the National Farmers' Union, Cheshire farmers discussed the problem and I was delegated to take a resolution to the county meeting of the National Farmers' Union. We wanted the Union to make representation to the government for immediate action on the use of the live vaccine. I raised the issue under 'any other business' and was told that it would be passed to the Poultry Committee to discuss. I was concerned that once the committee got hold of it the issue would be put on hold for weeks, and I asked that the matter be sent directly to London. Thankfully, the delegates were with me. They realised the seriousness of the situation and the matter was sent directly to the NFU headquarters.

Unfortunately, little happened politically at this point, but after this severe outburst of Fowl Pest, we were luckily never troubled with the disease again. Eventually in 1975 when the government advice changed, we were allowed to use the live vaccine rather than the dead one. This could be put in the hens' drinking water – a much easier and quicker process. Soon all the nights of 'poking' were in the past.

An Outbreak of Foot and Mouth

By the late 1960s, our herd of cattle consisted on forty Freisians. Bill Kerfoot, one of the gardeners who worked at Mere College, used to deliver our morning paper at milking time. One Monday morning in 1968, he dropped our paper in the porch as usual and then came over to the shippon to say hello. He would always announce his arrival by crowing like a cockerel. In fact, we used to call him 'Cock-a-doodle-doo.'

On this occasion, after the usual ritual, Bill announced that there had been a policeman barring his entry that morning to Bowdon View Farm, which was just the other side of Mere College. We asked him what he was doing there. 'Ah well,' said Bill knowingly, 'they have Foot and Mouth Disease.' 'What!' We all shouted, aghast, and bundled poor Bill out of the yard.

This was the beginning of a very worrying period. Apparently, the Allens at Bowdon View Farm had sent for Ken Whalley that Sunday. He had suspected Foot and Mouth and had contacted the Ministry of Agriculture vets who confirmed it on Sunday night. We were soon awash with disinfectant. The advice being given was that for a farm to become infected, there had to be contact or transmission on the wheels of lorries, people's feet or maybe even by birds or wild animals. It was not thought at that time that Foot and Mouth disease could be transmitted in the air by the wind.

Spring at last. The first days out in the fields for the cows at Yew Tree Farm after being indoors for the winter, 2007.

The whole procedure of slaughter and burial was a very clinical one. Some cattle from Holly House Farm (which could be seen from the entrance to Bowdon View Farm) were included. The machines burying the cattle moved away on Tuesday night – mission accomplished. It was a very worrying time, but different from future outbreaks in that everybody had confidence in the way the authorities were trying to control it. In the areas in which we lived, there were just those two outbreaks. Nobody ever worked out the physical connection that linked the two farms.

As soon as the infected farms had been controlled, Yew Tree Farm was visited by a Ministry vet – a man of experience who had seen many cattle with the disease in the past when he had worked on infected farms. He was from New Zealand and had come to Britain especially to help with outbreak. As we walked around the fields inspecting the cattle, the vet claimed that this strain of Foot and Mouth was a lot more virulent than any he had experienced before.

After we had walked all around the farm, the man from the Ministry asked me if we had any heifers. These were on a field across the A50 and within 100 yards of where the Bowdon cattle had been buried. I had deliberately kept this part of the herd back from inspection till last and I took a bit of delight in telling the vet where they were. He didn't appreciate my sense of humour and immediately said that if he had known that there had been cattle in that field so close to the infected farm, they would have been included in the slaughter. In the circumstances, he said that they had to remain on that field for the foreseeable future.

All our cattle were then inspected on a daily basis. After a week, I was instructed to house the milking cattle all the time (rather than just at night as I had been doing). I protested and said that that there was valuable grass outside for them to eat during the daytime. I also reminded the vet that the opinion at the time was that Foot and Mouth was not an airborne disease. But my protests were to no avail. I was told that I would be issued with an order. The vet said that he wasn't convinced in any case that the theories about the way the disease spread were correct. The inspection continued for about fourteen days (this is the usual infection period of the disease). As we were in a restricted area, we couldn't move the heifers from across the road even though they had eaten up all the grass over there and had nothing to eat.

Still a dairy farm in 2007.

We had to take food to the heifers for many weeks. Two of the heifers had calved – they had been crossed with an Aberdeen Angus – and the calves were two weeks old before we were allowed to move them. Even then, we had to apply for a so-called 'Movement Order.' We couldn't walk the cattle across the main road, but had to order a cattle wagon especially for the move. On the day of the move, my friend Prickle arrived slightly early to help out: the Ministry vet was late. We had the transport and got some gates in place to guide the cattle into the wagon. Considering they had never been loaded before, they did remarkably well – except for the two calves who got through the hedge onto a field that belonged to Bowdon View Farm. They began running around like wild deer. I was terrified that the man from the Ministry would arrive and catch them in what had been designated 'infected' territory.

After a good run around on the manure that had been spread on the day of the outbreak, the calves started to miss their mothers. Meanwhile, the mothers, who had already been loaded onto the cattle wagon, were showing their maternal instinct and bellowing their heads off. Hearing this noise, the calves eventually came back onto home ground and made their way to the gate where the wagon was. Prickle and I captured them with two superb rugby tackles and they were then securely fastened into the wagon. This was a situation in which I wished I had the lassooing expertise of a North American cowboy.

When the Ministry vet appeared, he apologised for being late. We told him that we had managed quite well and didn't refer to the episode with the calves. In fact, it probably wasn't the first time these young animals had strayed: new-born calves often go walkabouts after their first feed. What the vet's attitude would have been if he had known of these exploits can only be guessed at!

The Runaway Bull

One of the jobs Father insisted on continuing to do, even in his old age, was looking after the farm bull. There was a trough near the door of the pen into which he put the corn feed. Whilst the bull was eating, Father would put some hay at the far end of the pen in order to bed the area where the bull would lie down. This had happened every evening for years without any trouble. But, there is always an exception to the rule. One evening, perhaps the bull's appetite wasn't as good as it usually was. Before we knew it, the animal had got out of the door of the pen and was heading off down the A50.

To control a bull and get it back home, you need a lot of expertise and lot of luck. Eventually, we managed to turn the bull back towards the farm by getting past it in a van and driving towards it. We also had the bright idea of putting the cows out in the field. Once the bull saw them, we opened the gate and he ran towards them. Finally we got him back in his pen. After that, we always had two people on hand to keep an eye on the bull.

There didn't seem to be any pattern to how that outbreak of Foot and Mouth progressed. We just did as we were directed, using vast amounts of disinfectant and not associating with other people. I never read the Northumberland Report on the outbreak, but I did come across two published pieces of information on the disease sometime later. One said that the first outbreak that time had been near to Oswestry and that it had spread out fan-like with the prevailing wind – so much for the old theory! The other was that a lot of the disinfectant that we had been using was in fact incapable of killing the infection. Yew Tree Farm had been very fortunate indeed to miss the epidemic.

Fire at Old Farm

Farm fires are disasters that every person in the countryside can do without. Usually, they start in barns containing hay and straw. From my experience, electric faults are usually the cause. Leaky roofs can often contribute to the problem as water and electricity definitely don't mix. Then there are the mice that seem to have an appetite for the plastic coating on wires. When a mouse gnaws through a wire, the resulting flash can cause disastrous results – especially for the mouse!

Uncle Frank once had a fire up at the Bingo at Old Farm. This was a farm building that was set away from the main farm. It had originally been part of a nearby farm – Walnut Tree – which was occupied by a couple with a son of school age. In the Bingo, there were straw bales weighing about 112lbs each. Uncle Frank had sold most of his bales that year but there were a few left from the bottom of the pile that had suffered damage from the damp floor. These were ideal for school children to make dens and tunnels in. The boy next door had probably spent many happy hours in there with his friends and Uncle Frank no doubt knew what was happening and accepted the fact that this was common practice for children in the country.

Unfortunately, one night, the boy built a campfire in the Bingo which got out of control. His mother phoned the fire brigade and rang Uncle Frank to report the disaster. For a fire of that small size, the firemen didn't connect up with a fire hydrant, they just used the water from the tank in their vehicle. Uncle Frank looked at the fire engine and remarked (as he always did on such occasions): 'she comes with a bellyful and they daren't take any home!' The flames were soon put out, but the firemen continued to saturate the place. Uncle Frank was annoyed because as far as he was concerned, there was still a lot of valuable straw left in the bales. He said afterwards that there were only twelve bales in the Bingo, but that the fire brigade had sent thirteen firemen. He reckoned that they hadn't even got one each to work on!

Rabbits

I was familiar with breeding cattle and poultry, but rabbits were something altogether new to me. They came into my life by accident really. One night in 1969, the doorbell at the farmhouse rang as I was having my tea and a young woman stood in the doorway. She said that her name was Thyme and that she had a business proposition to put to me. She had heard that we had an empty shippon that we had just taken over at nearby Goodier's Green Farm and she wanted to rent it from me. The idea was that she would breed rabbits in it, for meat. She was very confident in her proposal and it was obvious that she had done her homework.

Rabbit on the Menu

Breeding rabbits was becoming a very popular activity in Cheshire in the 1970s. There was a local entrepreneur who would set you up in business. He would provide the cages, the breeding stock, and food troughs, and then he would market the rabbits you had reared. There was apparently a ready market for rabbit meat in the London hotels. This, of course, was far more succulent meat than the wild rabbit pie I was used to eating.

It was true that I had a shippon that we were not using and the idea of some extra income was of interest to me. Thyme made me a firm offer of a pound per week in rent to be paid in two instalments. We would have a book that I would sign on payment. I was a bit taken aback when Thyme took out a writing pad and drew up a tenancy agreement which I then had to sign. I pointed out that the agreements should cut both ways with the tenant being just as responsible a person as the landlord. She said that this was not the case – as in her opinion, it was landlords who were unscrupulous and dishonest.

Thyme was young and enthusiastic and I was impressed by her. It wasn't long before the rabbits were breeding and, of course, all the requisites for the business filled the shippon. For a while, the exercise seemed to be successful, but then, as is the case with all livestock being bred intensively, disease entered the picture. In this case it was infectious diarrhoea. I became aware that there were some problems and that not everything was going according to plan or to budget. One day I was a bit alarmed when I heard a calf bleating from inside the shippon. I enquired what was happening and was told that Thyme had now decided that she was going to keep cattle instead of rabbits. The animals would, of course, need straw and hay. We came to an agreement, though not in writing, that she would help herself to hay and straw from a nearby Dutch barn and that she would keep a record of what she used.

The rabbits disappeared and the number of cattle increased. I said to Thyme one day that she would have to get some land for grazing the cattle. A boyfriend appeared on the scene. More calves were being reared and Thyme rented some land from Edward Ford at High Legh for grazing. At one of our meetings when she paid her rent and a sum for the hay and straw she had used, I was told that she and her boyfriend were hoping to rent a council farm at Goostrey. I wrote a character assessment for the two of them to Cheshire County Council to support their application. This wasn't a problem for me as they were both working in jobs. Thyme paid me the compliment that she had never met as fair a landlord as me before. I certainly found Thyme unusual but I never doubted her honesty or integrity. After a while, she changed her name (maybe she married) and she had a child. After a little while longer, she and her husband had their council farm and two children.

The first I knew that anything had gone wrong was when I saw Thyme's husband in about 1973. He told me that Thyme had gone off, taking the two children with her. The rumour was that she had taken a job plucking turkeys at a local farm and had seen a gamekeeper through a haze of feathers across the room. She had fallen passionately in love with him. I'm not sure this was true, as I found out later that she had actually gone off alone in the van with the two children, the dog, a cat and a goat. Some people said she had gone to take up a job in Scotland. In fact, the reverse was true. She was actually housekeeping and helping with the milking on a farm in the south-west.

Thyme's business had foundered because she had been operating on borrowed money. This hadn't mattered as long as her stock values were increasing and keeping the bank manager happy. But once they weren't, she ran into difficulties. Farming had been stable during the war years and had kept profitable with deficiency payments that were paid by the government when the market price came down below the cost of production. These payments carried on until we joined the Common Market. Now the situation was different with threshold prices to stop food coming into the country below the stated price. If there was a glut of some agricultural produce, there was official buying of produce into intervention stores to raise the market price. In the case of corn, the price was kept high. Thyme found that it cost so much to feed the cattle that she could hardly make a profit.

The Prime Minister, Ted Heath, thought that the Common Market was the salvation of everything, but like most politicians, in my opinion, he made mistakes. In Britain, there was still free entry for agricultural produce from some countries, but no intervention buying of meat was put into place. The result was that – especially in the case of beef – the price crashed. Indeed, all cattle prices were reduced with disastrous results. I knew established beef farmers who were having a terrible time. Our Farmers' Union secretary, Robin Jones, took MPs around farms that were very badly affected. One local beef farmer who had been a wheeler and dealer all his life – and whom you would have thought could have handled anything – was admitted into the local mental institution because of it all.

Thyme's problem was on a smaller scale but I felt sorry for her. She too had been a victim of the agricultural policies of the early 1970s.

TEN

More Country Characters: Farmers, Tramps and Vicars

The countryside is as much about the characters that inhabit it as it is about animals and the natural world. Here are just a few longer portraits of some of the acquaintances, friends, advisors and sparring partners that I have known over the years.

The Texel Man

One of the most colourful characters in the local agricultural community was 'the Texel man' (so called because he had established a fine flock of Texel Sheep). He wasn't born in this country, but came here as a displaced person, probably from the Ukraine, to work on a farm in Cheshire at the end of the war. Even many years later, he hadn't quite mastered the intricacies of the English language, but that never stopped him from expressing a great sense of principle and a remarkable sense of humour.

The Texel man was always after a bargain. He once bought a baler at Chelford Market. The machine had a bale of hay correctly tied inside it as if to demonstrate that it worked properly. But when the Texel Man got it home, the baler refused to tie any knots. Something was wrong with a part of the machine known as the 'knotter'. The knotters on this type of baler were not considered reparable and usually you had to scrap them and buy a new one. But the Texel Man had paid good money for his machine and was determined to sort the problem out.

He went to the agricultural machinery agent who stocked the knotters and was told that the price to replace the faulty knotter would be £400. This was ridiculous as the Texel Man had only paid £250 for the baler in the first place. Understandably, he was getting angry, when suddenly the man in the store noticed that a loose pin had dropped out of the machine onto the counter top. 'This is your problem,' he exclaimed. Without the pin, the tying mechanism in the knotter would not revolve as it should do. In the end it cost the Texel Man just a few pence to replace the knotter – his perseverance, and his sense of principle, had paid off.

The Careful Farmer

A local farmer known for being a little careful with his money was taken into hospital for keyhole surgery to correct pain in his knee. The Texel man considered the situation for short while and then said, 'Operation not necessary. Tell him stop wearing money belt – this will reduce the pressure.'

The Texel man and his daughter also ran a small farm shop. Even selling potatoes at your gate can have its problems because people will sometimes complain about the quality of the potatoes. The Texel Man reckoned that what British housewives really wanted was a potato that remained whole no matter how long it was boiled. He would comment with exasperation, 'They put potato in pan. They turn up heat. They have screaming kids or they go watching television. Bubble, bubble, bubble, bubble. They go back to stove. They find mush in the bottom of pan!' When one lady complained about the potatoes she had bought from the Texel Man's shop, she received the reply: 'Nothing the matter with potatoes: cook that is wrong.'

I got the impression that the Texel Man had seen many of the problems of this world in his time and had now finally found stability with his sheep and his shop. He was certainly one of the most respected people in the area and often enjoyed a game of dominoes with friends. People reported crying with laughter after having spent an evening playing dominoes with him.

Bill Davies

Bill Davies was a farmer from Ashley whom I had first met at Chelford Market. He had two farms: one that he owned in Nottingham and a rented farm in Ashley, Cheshire which he had no intention of giving up. He used to bring produce up to Chelford from his farm in Nottingham on a motor lorry. Later on he bought a third farm in Crowley, Cheshire.

Nosey Farmers

The trouble with farmers is that they are always 'farming over the hedge': that is, they are inquisitive about – if not a little envious of – other people's farms. I know one family with some land a little way from home. They use four different routes to get to it, just so that they can look over the hedges and see what is going in on in neighbouring farms. They claim that they are using a one-way system because of the narrow lanes, but I don't believe it.

One day, while Bill was moving a wheeled excavator to his farm in Crowley, a front wheel fell off his vehicle. On inspection, he discovered that the studs had worked loose and he had to call for some bolts to secure the wheel and complete the journey. He blamed himself, saying that if hadn't been so interested in what was going on over the hedges, he would have seen the wheel wobbling and anticipated the problem. He thought he would get a good rollicking from his family when they found out.

Funny things kept happening to Bill Davies. He once had a heifer that had calved. As is quite typical of newborn calves, this one had gone walkabout after its first feed from its mother. The calves from one farm that I used to know often ended up in a rhubarb patch in a nearby garden and go to sleep. On this occasion, Bill's calf had found its way into a neighbouring farmyard and got itself inside a loosebox (or so Bill believed). The farmer's son didn't share Bill's opinion and proclaimed that the calf in the loosebox belonged to his father. Bill sent two helpers to the farm to try to retrieve the calf whilst he went to fetch the mother of the calf in a trailer.

The two helpers got a far from welcoming reception from the farmer's son. He was cutting string for tying up sacks and the knife he was using was apparently the size of a machete! As the young man cut the string, he waved the knife about in the air in a threatening manner. At this point, Bill arrived with the mother cow. The calf was let out and, luckily for Bill, there was an instant bond of recognition between the two animals. It was only then that the farmer's son put the knife down; he had to agree that the calf had found its rightful owner.

Asleep in a Window

Bill Davies used to take his wife into Knutsford to have her hair done. Whilst she was in the hairdresser's chair, he would wander off to look around the town. One afternoon, he fell asleep in a chair in the window of a furniture shop, much to the amusement of the passers by!

Unfortunately all good lives eventually come to an end. When Bill died, the church at Ashley was full of people paying their last respects to one of agriculture's greatest characters. The funeral address was given by Bill's daughter, Lorna, who was a lecturer at Myerscough College in Lancashire. It was one of the best I have ever heard. It was a true reflection of Bill's life and made reference to all his antics and experiences. The congregation were rolling in the aisles. I suppose Lorna got some of her expertise at public speaking from her job, but some of it also came from her mother (who was my best friend Ted Whittaker's sister) and from her father, Bill himself. Most funerals are solemn occasions, but I came away from this one elated and proud to have known such a wonderful family.

Tom Bostock

One of the most memorable local characters was Tom Bostock. He ran nearby Daisy Bank farm virtually single-handed. In fact, I don't remember him ever having had a worker to help him. Tom was a gentle person, and very deliberate with his speech. Sometimes, if you asked him a question, you could work out what he was going to say before he finished saying it. I used to enjoy listening to him talking to my parents. One wet summer in the 1950s, Mother said, 'It's very bad harvest weather, Mr Bostock.' After a considerable delay, Tom came out with one of his gems. 'Aye Missus Wright it is, but we have seen it all before.' This sort of reply inevitably killed the conversation.

One-man farms are very much at risk if the farmer has the misfortune to be ill. At one point, Tom had difficulty swallowing. This and various other symptoms caused the doctor a lot of concern. It turned out that he had tetanus, or 'lockjaw', as it is more commonly known. Tom was in hospital for many weeks, and some of the time was under complete sedation. At this time, quite strangely, I knew of three people all suffering from the same complaint. One of these men had supposedly contracted the problem by spiking his arm with the stalk of a Michaelmas Daisy while clearing up his garden. Unfortunately, this man died, but the other two thankfully made full recoveries. Whilst Tom was ill, the locals rallied round and helped out on the farm. His daughter took charge and reduced the number of livestock because, as she put it, 'Charity only lasts a fortnight.'

Tom was once at a farm sale where the cattle ring was constructed out of bales of straw. A frisky heifer jumped over into the crowd of interested buyers who ran back a considerable distance to escape it. Long after the animal was gone, Tom was heard to say, 'Now then chaps, we'd better move back a bit'. I used to enjoy meeting up with Mr Bostock (as I always called him out of respect) and I looked forward to his protracted conversation. I always asked him how he was and the reply was always the same, 'Tidy lad, tidy.'

Amos Gould

There are some characters who just keep turning up in your life no matter how much you try to avoid them. One of these was Amos Gould, a local vagrant who lived for many years in a shack on the lane which runs down the side of Yew Tree Farm. Dobb Lane is a wooded bridle path between Mere and High Legh, it was mentioned in the Domesday Book and it certainly has quite a lot of recent history. People have committed suicide there and – from the goings on I have witnessed – some people's lives probably started there! It is now a Site of Special Scientific Interest, but it has always been enjoyed by ramblers and nature lovers. We used to use Dobb Lane to gain access to some of the fields on Yew Tree Farm. At one time, we farmed some land at High Legh at Hobbs Hill Farm (the home of Uncle Peter Cook who used to kill our pigs during the war) and we had to drive our cattle regularly along Dobb Lane to and from that land.

One day in the 1960s, I noticed something strange on the Lane - some branches had been woven to form a screen and a kind of wooden roof had been constructed. At first, I didn't think much about it as I knew that there were some men in the area who liked to go pigeon shooting and I thought that it was probably one of their hides. It wasn't until I caught sight of the familiar face of Amos Gould that I realised that someone was actually living there.

Amos Turned Outdoors

Before living in the shack, Amos resided with his wife and family in the Tabley area. He had first a farm cottage and later a council house and he worked for Cheshire County Council driving a loading shovel. Apparently, he started to live rough after he had a disagreement with his wife. It was said that on returning from the Second World War, he had realised that there was one child more in the family than he could account for. This, as can be imagined, led to repeated arguments and worse. In fact, Amos had a mark on his forehead from a wound where Mrs Gould had hit him. People said that she had used the blunt end of an axe, and more than a few remarked that she should perhaps have hit him with the other end!

It wasn't long before some well-meaning person managed to drive an old van up to Amos's shelter and, for a while, he lived in that. He would call on Mother at the farm for hot water for his brew and for his cooking needs. Sometimes, he would work on one of the local farms on a piecework basis. People said that he was all right if you were working alongside him, but, left to his own devices, he would soon have a scam going. At one time, my friend J.P. took Amos on to pull up common turnips. At the end of the day, he would report on how many hampers he had filled and J.P. would pay him per hamper. Unfortunately, when J.P. went to empty the hampers into bags, he found that the bottom of each one had been filled with foliage and that there were just a few turnips on the top!

Amos only worked when he felt like it, which annoyed me because he was quite intelligent and was certainly physically capable of holding down a job. I made these points clear to a person from Social Security who came enquiring about him one day. I couldn't believe it when her reply was, 'Oh yes, but he is such a loveable rogue!' When he wasn't working, Amos wasn't quite destitute, as he had what he said was a pension from being injured during the Second World War. Whether the bit of money he had was in fact from a war pension or was just social security, I don't know, but it was paid on a Monday. This usually meant that Amos went to a pub on Monday night and then slept in the British Legion or the Salvation Army Hostel in Warrington.

In time, Amos built himself a bigger shelter with a stove in it. It wasn't particularly waterproof, and after very heavy rain, you would see his bedding hanging out to dry. The local authority, Bucklow Rural District Council, made attempts to house Amos, as did Social Services, but to no avail. They had a flat for him in Sale (near Manchester), but he wouldn't go. I don't know whether he ever got himself into prison, but he certainly got himself into old people's homes for Christmas. He would do his famous fainting act in some public place or shop and Emergency Services would be contacted. If the police got there first, Amos's ploy would be rumbled, and he would be given a prod and told to get up – much to the alarm of members of the public who didn't know him.

Dobb Lane in 2007: the glade in which Amos Gould lived in a range of different types of accommodation under the leaning oak tree.

Between 1968 and 1972, there were a spate of fires especially in the High Legh and Crowley areas. Amos was the prime suspect. Two detectives once asked me whether I had seen Amos lately. I knew there had been a fire on the Monday night and I told the two detectives to check Amos's alibis. Monday was his drinking day, and he had probably been sleeping off the after effects in one of his usual haunts. Whether or not he had started the fire was another matter. I saw Amos some days later. He seemed very pleased with himself and said that he had been helping the police with their enquiries.

Then one night, there was another fire in Millington. A man had been seen in the area just before the fire started riding a bicycle. The police went to visit Amos in his shack in the middle of the night. To their surprise, they found another man there. He was a friend of Amos's who worked at Goodiers Green Farm on Hoo Green Lane. This chap lived in a hostel at Tabley with other men with learning difficulties. That night, when the police arrived, Amos was in his bed. The other man suddenly grabbed the centre post of the hut, gave it an almighty wrench and escaped out of the door just as the roof came down on the police and Amos.

A lady who lived down Wrenshot Lane, opposite our farm, told me how she had been woken up by a noise in the middle of that night. On putting on the light, she saw a terrified man at her bedroom door. The police were soon on their way and the man was arrested. It turned out to be the man from Goodiers Green Farm and he was soon standing trail accused of arson. Amos was called as a witness. The barrister asked him, 'Now Mr Gould, What time was it when all this happened?

'Two o'clock,' was the answer.

'Have you got a watch, Mr Gould?' said the barrister.

'No,' replied Amos.

'Then how do you know it was two o'clock?' said the barrister.

'Because every night at two o'clock, the old owl hoots twice and the dog fox walks past my door,' replied Amos. Apparently the courtroom was in uproar.

Even after Amos had been down Dobb Lane for about seven years, his living conditions were still very primitive. One day as I was travelling along Hoo Green Lane and passing the far end of Dobb Lane, I noticed a wooden shed left on the side of the road. On Friday night I went out on my egg-and-potato round (selling produce from Yew Tree Farm) and one of my customers, a widow, who sold tools and household goods, told me that some do-gooders who were concerned about Amos's living conditions had brought the shed as replacement accommodation for him. In fact, they were coming on Sunday morning to carry it up Dobb Lane and erect it. As I owned the land on one side of Dobb Lane I was very interested in, not to mention irritated by, this proposal. The lady confided in me that Amos had recently bought an axe and a saw from her, but that she had not been paid.

On Sunday mornings, I often went for a drive around the local area to look at my crops and cattle. Sometimes, I visited a neighbour to discuss business or put the world to rights. On this occasion, however, I decided there was a situation that needed sorting out. I arrived at the bottom of Dobb Lane at the same time as the helpers who were intent on giving Amos a more luxurious shelter. They were waiting for Amos to decide exactly where they should erect his new home. I asked the man in charge on whose authority he was erecting the shed. He replied that his father had shooting rights on the estate and that this was their land. I had to disappoint the young man and said that the estate only owned a narrow strip on the High Legh side: I owned the rest. When he protested, I invited him to accompany me home to inspect the deeds.

The young man seemed convinced that Amos was a deserving case and said that I should give him and his friends permission to erect the shed on the land owned by our family. I told him that I couldn't give them permission even if I agreed that Amos was a deserving case (which, incidentally, I didn't): I would need planning permission from the local council. I also mentioned the widow who hadn't been paid for the axe and the saw.

Whilst we were talking, we heard the rattle of clogs coming towards us. It was Amos on his way to help. The young man took Amos aside and they had a conversation for about ten minutes. When the young man came back to me he said that Amos agreed that he owed the money and that he would pay it off the next week. The young man said that the group of helpers would hold off erecting the shed for another week in the hope that I would change my mind.

The next Friday night on my egg-and-potato round, I went to see the widow again. She said that Amos still hadn't paid his debts. I was wondering what to do about the shed, whether or not I should relent and agree to improving Amos's living conditions. On the Saturday, however, I noticed that the shed had disappeared. I wondered whether the group had come early and erected it. Thankfully, sometimes when you fear the worst, it doesn't happen. The shed was never actually erected. Believe it or not, Amos had found a buyer for it and pocketed the money. No doubt he used it to fuel his passion for alcohol!

It wasn't long after this that Amos completely disappeared from the area. He didn't say farewell, not even to Mother who had made him warm drinks. What had happened was that local government reorganisation had taken place and Macclesfield Borough Council had become the local authority for the area. Amos had been offered – and had accepted – a bungalow on the Weston estate in Macclesfield. He originated from Bollington and so found this new suggestion from the council more acceptable than the offer in Sale.

The Unmarked Tins

When Amos left Dobb Lane, my sister Joyce was rather relieved as it meant that she would no longer be asked to warm up tins for him in pans of boiling water. She had never enjoyed this as she hadn't known what the contents were. They had never had any labels on!

Amos didn't quite disappear from our lives. Kathleen's father and mother used to come over to see us most Saturdays from Macclesfield. They reported that they had seen Amos a few times in and around the town. On one occasion they had gone to buy ham for our tea in a local butcher's shop. There was a dog outside which had been tied to a downspout outside a pub on Mill Lane. Apparently whilst my parents-in-law were in the butchers, they noticed a male dog giving the tethered dog a lot of attention. A lady who had also witnessed this had come into butcher's shop and expressed her disgust at what was going on. The butcher started to run a bowl of cold water to pour over the animals to separate them. But the lady became very indignant and said that this was not the way to deal with the matter: the RSPCA must be called for. Of course, when the RSPCA man arrived, all he did was ask for a bucket of cold water to pour over the dogs. Somebody realised that the owner of the dog must be inside the pub. Very soon, the owner did appear at the door of the pub – it was Amos!

Amos's lifestyle went on causing concern for the authorities. He continued to saw, split and sell firewood from his home on the estate. On reaching retirement age, he got a job as a night watchman in one of the Macclesfield mills but he was still good at getting voluntary admissions into local hospitals and institutions. I have had many conversations with local police officers from all over the Macclesfield Borough over the years and they have all had stories to tell about Amos.

Some years later, I was driving into Macclesfield when I saw a motorised buggy coming in the opposite direction. The driver looked older than I remembered him, but he still had the same mane of strong hair blowing in the wind. It was Amos. That was the last time I ever saw him.

Vicars

I had a Christian upbringing in the family and at High Legh Village School where we had to recite all the articles of the Christian Faith. We understood that the Ten Commandments were the basis of a decent society, though some of us struggled with the one about not committing adultery. It interfered with our natural urges! Joking aside, a succession of local vicars have played a significant part in my life over the years.

Graveyards

Local graveyards are very important places. Country people often have many generations of their family buried there. They take wreaths at Christmas and flowers on birthdays and at Easter and they tend the graves with love and care. I know that I have occasionally popped down to Rostherne Village to brighten up the family graves before relatives from overseas have visited them.

The local graveyard was getting full and people were buying plots in advance. A chap I knew called Tom had bought his wife a plot as a Christmas present. The following year, some inquisitive person asked Tom what he was buying Mary for Christmas this time. 'Nothing', he replied, 'She hasn't used last year's present yet!'

The Reverend Oliver
The first local vicar I remember was the Revd John Oliver at St John's church, High Legh. From his dialect, I guess he came from Northern Ireland. Mother used to take me to church when I was a child and he used to frighten me. It was all right when we were doing something such as singing hymns or saying prayers, but I found it difficult to sit still during the sermon especially as Mother would only ever bring one sweet with her for me to suck.

During the sermon, Johnny Oliver, as we used to call him, would get very excited and wave his arms about. He nearly fell head first out of the pulpit, so enthusiastic was he about his sermon. I'm afraid that at that age, I didn't understand his theology, but Mother seemed to think that he knew what he was talking about. I used to beg her to bring more than one sweet – his sermons were so long.

The Reverend Hughes

St John's, High Legh, hadn't been registered for marriages and didn't have a graveyard. St Mary's Rostherne was the mother church and all the marriages and funerals took place there. When the Revd John Oliver retired in the late 1930s, it was no longer possible to sustain a priest at High Legh and we came under the authority of the vicar of Rostherne. The Revd John Hughes took the spiritual needs of both his parishes very seriously and conducted services in both places. On a Sunday, he would conduct early matins at 9.15 a.m. at High Legh giving himself time to return to Rostherne for morning service at 10.30. On Sunday evenings, he was at Rostherne at 6.30 and at High Legh at 8 p.m. for evensong. As a result of all his to-ing and fro-ing, there was always an undercurrent between the people of Rostherne and the people of High Legh about sharing the vicar. The people of Rostherne thought that their vicar was being asked to do too much. They were probably right, but there ought to be compassion in religion!

   The Revd Hughes had a young family who came to church with him and went to school at Altrincham with my sister Joyce. Most Sunday mornings, the vicar would stop to pick up my sister Joyce and her friend Molly and take them to church. He drove a Morris 8. Because we had one as well, Joyce knew where the gears were. She said that the vicar was not a terribly good driver. When he used to take her to church, she noticed that although he knew where reverse was, he would use any of the three forward gears indiscriminately for going forward!

The Cock and Hen Choir

The Revd Hughes used the lifts he gave people to recruit them for the church choir. Some such choirs are very sophisticated with different people singing different parts. At High Legh it wasn't like that at all. The vicar called it a 'cock and hen choir' – they just needed someone to get them going. There was a girl whose surname was 'Toobey.' One morning, the humorous vicar was deliberating whether or not to keep her in the choir and intoned, in his best Shakespearean voice, 'Toobey or not Toobey, that is the question.'

The Reverend Haworth

The Revd Hughes died relatively young after being elevated to the position of canon. At this point, the parish of High Legh was joined with that of Tabley and a new vicar, the Revd Haworth was assigned the job of looking after both parishes. He was a new type of vicar, a man who had come into the ministry after being a successful captain of industry. He was a very good man but used to being the boss.

   I ended up on the parochial Church Council at this time and finances were always a problem. The parish magazine was in trouble as the advertising revenue was not keeping up with the publishing costs. We had a recruitment drive to find more local firms interested in advertising. When I looked at the magazine closely, I realised that the message from the vicar was taking up a lot of space. Thinking I was being helpful, I suggested that he should write his speech to fill up the space that was left after the adverts had gone in. Perhaps unsurprisingly, the Revd Haworth told me in no uncertain terms that he was not writing a letter but a spiritual message and that he would take up all the space that he needed!

St John's church, High Legh. The boulders in the foreground supposedly came from Cumbria and are glacial deposits from the last ice age.

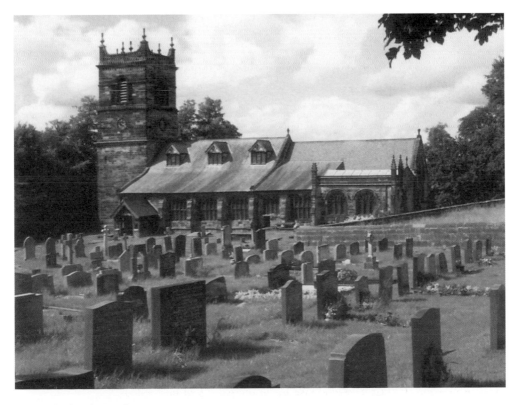

St Mary's church, Rostherne.

Uncle Frank and the Papal Smoke

In the early 1950s, Uncle Frank was working in a field next to a large country house surrounded not only by a high hawthorn hedge, but also by a boarded fence so that he couldn't see anything at all in the garden next door. The gardener had a good fire burning with plenty of smoke billowing up. At that time, the pope had recently passed away and a new one was being elected. Everybody was enthralled by the way popes were chosen with all the cardinals congregating in the Sistene chapel and no message going to the outside world until the right-coloured smoke came out through the chapel chimney. The papal selection was taking a long time and was featured on continuing news bulletins. Eventually, the smoke from the garden was too much for Uncle Frank. He shouted over the fence, 'You got a new pope yet?'

Mr Bend and Uncle Frank – Church Wardens

Mr Bend – a local gamekeeper – was one of the church wardens at St John's, High Legh. He was very well respected in the parish as gamekeepers were treated with the same respect as policemen by the local community. Mr Bend needed a helper and he asked Uncle Frank to join him. There was a big difference in stature between the two men. Mr Bend was small and stooped – and at that time in his life took small steps. Uncle Frank, on the other hand, was an ex-grenadier guardsman who had done sentry duty at Buckingham Palace. I suppose Uncle Frank with his training and his best suit used to get carried away with the ceremonial in church. Certainly, he used to rear up to his full height, chest forward and shoulders back and set off for the altar with massive strides, just as if was marching along in the Changing of the Guard. It was amusing to watch Mr Bend having to take two strides to his every one to keep up.

A Reluctant Santa

At the church Christmas Fayre in High Legh Village Hall, there was always a Father Christmas. Originally, my only contribution to this event was to provide the Wellingtons for whoever played the part of this genial old gentleman, but before long, the local ladies wanted me to wear them. I never felt comfortable. First of all, Father Christmases need a fairy to take the money and introduce the children into the grotto. My fairy was a very nice lady but she was of somewhat advancing years. I had bag of presents for the girls and one for the boys. I suppose the job was all right as long as the children had their mothers with them and they could tell me who was who. The trouble was that when children came in unaccompanied, we didn't necessarily know which sex they were. So we had a bag of goodies for those that we weren't sure about and those who were too shy to tell you their name.

One little girl whom I knew very well confided in her mother after leaving the grotto that Father Christmas was in fact Uncle Walter. Her mother asked how she had arrived at that conclusion, thinking that she must have recognised the voice. 'It's his hands,' said the little girl. 'They're Uncle Walter's hands.'

I don't think I was cut out to be Father Christmas. It was one of the most harrowing jobs I have ever done and it was quite a relief when someone else took over the role and I could get back to milking the cows!

The Reverend Dean

In the 1970s, one of the vicars of the parishes of High Legh and Tabley. One of the vicars was the Revd Andrew Dean. He was the first one to insist that we called him by his Christian name rather than by his formal title. In the late 1960s, we used to visit church on a Sunday afternoon for family worship. Andrew was wonderful with the children, getting them involved in the service and explaining the gospel to them. Some of the children, perhaps more especially the boys, were there under duress and were not particularly religious, but Andrew was nearly always able to get them interested.

A Modern Parable

One harvest festival, the parable of the sower was being discussed. We got to the bit about the crop being choked with weeds, and the vicar asked the children what they would do in such a circumstance. I suppose for centuries, vicars had been asking this question and the answer had been the same, 'Pull the weeds out'. On this occasion, one bright little boy – evidently a farmer's son – said 'Spray them.'

Not everybody appreciated Andrew Dean's informality. He moved on to work in Astbury near Congleton. I was once delivering a load of straw over there and spoke to a man who was working in his garden. I mentioned the fact that our old vicar was working in his parish. This man had not been very impressed when his grandson had told him that he was allowed to call the vicar by his Christian name. He thought standards were slipping and that a vicar should command more respect.

Divine Help

The Revd Andrew Dean used to wear a roll-neck pullover which obscured his dog collar. Once he pulled over to help a lady whose car had broken down. He suggested that she open the bonnet whilst he took a look and he managed to solve the problem. The car started straight away and the woman looked at him and said, 'I don't know who you are but you must have been sent by Him from up above!'

ELEVEN

The Retirement of Uncle Frank and of the Claas Combine

Throughout this account, I have made many mentions of Mother's brother, Uncle Frank, who ran Old Farm, High Legh. When I was young I never warmed to Uncle Frank as I had done to his brother Charlie. This might have been because he once had a part in a play at High Legh as a policeman and I had been brought up to respect and fear the law. As I grew older, however, I grew to understand Uncle Frank better and I came to appreciate his dry sense of humour. He had a particular way with words which meant that you remembered what he said for a long time afterwards. Even now when we have a good spell of weather early in the year, I can hear Uncle Frank commenting that the sunshine should be 'bagged up and let loose in June' when it would be needed for haymaking.

Uncle Frank's Ladies

Uncle Frank came from an age before motorised vehicles were a usual sight on the roads. He used to refer to all vehicles – from tractors and fire engines to cars – as if they were female and had personalities. As a child, I used to cycle home from school past Old Farm. One afternoon as I approached the junction, where I usually turned to go up the hill, Uncle Frank was coming down with his cart. A post van snaked past his horses, round the bend, and narrowly missed us. Uncle Frank shouted after it, 'steady on you little red bitch!'

In the late 1960s, Uncle Frank was getting older. For a long time, there had been no deterioration in his hearing – he could even hear when people mumbled and didn't speak clearly – but his eyesight eventually started to fail. He wasn't a reader, but he did get a daily newspaper and a weekly farming paper. The first indication that his eyesight was deteriorating was when he told Aunty Bertha that the printing in the newspaper was 'trashy'. Uncle Frank and Aunty Bertha were brother and sister, but in some respects they were like a married couple. She knew that he would never agree to go for an eye test, so eventually she secured an appointment without telling him. Then, on one of their weekly shopping trips into the village of Lymm, she escorted Uncle Frank in the direction of the opticians.

According to Uncle Frank, he was having the usual tests done when the optician was called away by a phone call. Whilst he was left on his own, Uncle Frank noticed some pairs of glasses lying around. He started trying them on for size until he found a pair he could see better through. On the return of the optician, he announced, 'You don't need to bother any more, I've found some that will do the job!' The optician gave him a severe reprimand and told him that being fitted with glasses was a very delicate and scientific operation. Uncle Frank accepted the advice and waited for his glasses. The pair he eventually received were 'all right,' he said, but he always maintained that they were not a bit better than the ones he had originally tried on.

Uncle Frank in his retirement
with his bicycle. Behind him is
the shed that he used to refer to
as 'the office'.

Many of the shopkeepers in Lymm must have found Uncle Frank a difficult customer. He
used to go to Bert Gray's barbers in Lymm for a trim. After cutting someone's hair, Bert would
put a dressing on to finish the job off. But when he reached for the bottle after cutting Uncle
Frank's hair, he was firmly told to 'put that bag muck away'. 'Bag muck' was a local term for
artificial fertilizer.

Uncle Frank on the Road

Uncle Frank had never driven a motor vehicle in his life. His only connection with the
internal combustion engine was when his friend, Steer Moss, encouraged him to have a go
on a motorbike. He gave him instructions on how to start off but didn't impress upon him
how to stop it! Needless to say, it wasn't long before Uncle Frank ended up in a hedge.

Eventually, in 1965 Uncle Frank decided it was time to retire. There was a row of cottages on
West Lane, High Legh, about half a mile away from Old Farm that had been built before the
Second World War. Uncle Frank and Aunty Bertha bought one of them. Three other retired
farmers already lived there and West Lane became known locally as 'the golden mile.'

The Sale of Old Farm

Uncle Frank and Aunty Bertha's home, Old Farm, had been the last farm in the area to be
farmed with horses. When it was sold in 1965, it was a nostalgic event. The place would no
longer be run as a farm. The house and buildings (together with a small area of land) were
sold off from High Legh Estate and the remaining land was let to other farmers. The sale was
quite successful, considering – or perhaps because of – the fact that most of the implements
were horse-drawn. Later, the wooden and corrugated iron buildings where my grandfather
had cut up his firewood and the little area that Aunty Bertha had called his 'playpen' were

demolished. The stable, shippon and lofts above were converted and became extra living accommodation attached to the house. Inside, some of the character of the house was retained, the old Fletcher-Russell black grate, for example, was kept.

Apart from his years in the Army in the First World War, Uncle Frank had never known anything else but life on the farm. Remarkably, however, he settled into retirement in the cottage in West Lane very well. He spent a lot of time in his garden shed and came to refer to it as 'the office'. He also had regular jaunts along the surrounding country lanes on his bicycle and his friend, Steer Moss, would take him for drives in the car around the countryside. Sometimes they would go shooting on farms they knew, or visit each others' houses and tell stories about their younger days. Aunty Bertha used to be amused by the way they spoke because they could never remember people's names or places and usually referred to them as 'thingamabob' or 'where-do-you-call-it?'

Work for the Lord

With his skills at hedge cutting and scything, Uncle Frank was soon in great demand helping people with their gardens. One day, he had been cutting grass around the St John's church in High Legh and was walking home when somebody asked him who he had been working for that day. He replied, 'Jesus.'

One Sunday morning in his retirement, I took Uncle Frank for a drive to Prescot, Lancashire to the farm of a man named Ted Hughes. Our stocks of old potatoes were exhausted, the new ones weren't yet ready and I needed a few extra bags of potatoes for my round on Friday night. Reg (one of the drivers) came to the gate to give me the potatoes I had ordered. He asked Uncle Frank how he was coping with his retirement. 'Very busy,' came the reply, 'in fact I'm thinking of taking on an apprentice!'

Aunty Bertha in her old age at Yew Tree Farm.

As for Aunty Bertha, she had far more time on her hands in her retirement. She would be seen out and about in her Morris Minor visiting local elderly people. She also enjoyed playing whist and sometimes she won prizes. One evening, she won a frozen chicken and brought it home, but Uncle Frank wasn't having any of it. He had seen enough of it thawing out in the bucket.

Uncle Frank's Appetite

Uncle Frank's had a lot of set ideas about food. He wouldn't eat soup, for example, since he reckoned it had no 'body' in it, and he complained that when you put a bun into the bowl it sailed round like a duck. He remembered with horror his time in the Army when 'bully beef' was the order of the day. If he was served with anything resembling this awful stuff, including corned beef, he refused to eat it. One day in his retirement, after his midday meal, he was sitting reading the paper when a woman sailed into the house announcing herself as 'Meals-on-Wheels'. She thrust a meal in what Uncle Frank referred to as a 'Dixie' in front of him, and with apologies for being late, said she hoped that Uncle Frank enjoyed the meal and turned to leave. Just before she reached the back door, Uncle Frank managed to impress upon her that she had got the wrong house. She should have been at the Wardells next door!

There were a lot of changes in High Legh at this time and I don't think that Uncle Frank was happy with all of them, though they certainly made the first years of his retirement interesting. A housing estate was being built around the chapel where he used to sing as a boy – though, thankfully, the chapel itself was preserved. East and West Hall at High Legh were being demolished, along with part of the Army camp built during the Second World War. The gardens where the famous missionary Robert Moffit had worked, along with the bothy where he lived, were being developed, and, as if that wasn't enough, the village cross mysteriously disappeared.

The other thing that occupied Uncle Frank's attention in his retirement was the appearance of the M56 motorway in 1973. This took up some of the land at Old Farm, and closed the road that went past West Lane, so that access was only from the Lymm end. The Golden Mile became a cul-de-sac and Uncle Frank's house was at the M56 end below the embankment for the motorway bridge. Eventually some steps were put in to allow for quick access. There is no nameplate there, but so memorable was my uncle that those steps are now known as the 'Frank Hulme' steps.

The March of Progress

Uncle Frank may have been upset about the changes that were taking place in his immediate vicinity, but, in the 1970s, the whole look of the Cheshire countryside changed. There was a vastly increased demand for produce and this meant that many smaller farms were amalgamated. The land was bought by local farmers whilst the extra farm houses were bought by city dwellers as second residences. In addition to this, new planning guidance regulations came out that stated that brick-built farm buildings could be converted into houses or put to business use. Other buildings were removed or used for garaging.

The larger quantities of produce brought about many other changes on the farms. Shippons became obsolete with cattle now being housed in much larger sheds. The old milk churns disappeared and were replaced by large milk tankers that went from farm to farm. Grain too was handled in bulk and 'dryers' were installed to ensure that it was stored correctly.

The threshing machine had long been replaced by the combine harvester, of course, but farmers in the 1970s and 1980s were competing with bigger and better models. As the driver of a combine harvester, you become attached to the machine during the harvest period. You spend long hours coaching it through the fields, especially in the wet years when the crop becomes tangled and laid flat. I was very fond and indeed proud of our first combine harvester but as the years went on and we had to keep updating the machine, my feelings about combining started to change.

The Matador, The Dominator and the Claas 106

We had started with a Matador Combine Harvester and had it from new until its retirement in a bed of nettles at the back of the farm. After this it was cannibalised for parts. The Matador was reliable and had given good service, but in 1983 I was looking for something better. The second machine I had was bigger with more horsepower. It had a new name to match – Dominator. I was rather disappointed with this machine in the field, however, as it performed in much the same way as the Matador. Both these machines had the same threshing mechanism, it was only the horse power and the length of the straw walker (an area for separating the grain from the straw), combined with the increased cutting width, that gave the Dominator its so-called 'increased capacity.'

Farm machines in general were getting bigger. Perhaps I had a rush of blood to the head, but in 1986 I decided it was time that we bought a third combine harvester. I contacted a dealer from the firm 'Claas' and after some discussion and much persuasion, I agreed to buy a combine of the Claas 106 variety. It arrived the next summer in plenty of time for the harvest and word got around the farming fraternity that Yew Tree Farm had a new combine. Very soon we had a full order book for its hire.

The new combine Claas 106. In the beginning it was the talk of the county.

The Luxurious Combine

Often combine harvesters can't be seen when they are working – all that is visible is a cloud of dust moving along, behind which a fresh row of newly threshed straw emerges. The driver of old-fashioned combine harvesters was unprotected and would get covered in dust and chaff. The new Claas 106 machine, by contrast, had a cab. This was luxury for me. It also had a comfortable seat that was fully adjustable, and soundproofing.

The Sad Demise of the Claas 106

In 1987, there was a prolonged wet spell and a lot of the crops were laid flat with sprouted ears. They were also tangled and matted with chickweed growing through because the effects of the residual sprays had worn off. The 'new lady', as Uncle Frank used to call the combine, certainly had a task on her hands.

That season marked the beginning of our difficulties with the combine harvester. First of all, there was the problem with the reel tines. They kept breaking off. This caused me some concern as I had never experienced a broken tine on a combine harvester before. By the end of the season, so many tines had broken off that combining a field was starting to feel like trying to comb your hair with a ruler.

Next there was the problem with the fan inside the cab. Occasionally it would stop working which meant that there was no air conditioning. Sometimes the cab felt like a greenhouse and there was no method of cooling it down except for driving along with the doors open which wasn't very practical. On one occasion when I was driving to Appleton with the trailer coupled up behind the combine, all the warning lights and warning bleepers came on for no particular reason. I couldn't understand what had happened as these mechanisms are only supposed to come on when the threshing mechanism is in gear and there is loss of speed on a shaft. I never found out the cause of this, although it happened on at least one other occasion.

The last job the Claas combine did that season was to harvest a field of oats. It made a very bad job of it. The crops were laid flat on the floor due to heavy rain and strong wind and there was chickweed covering most of the field. This was an organic crop, so no dessicant had been sprayed on the chickweed to kill it off. The whole thing was a mess. Even once I had managed to cut the crop, the threshing mechanism on the combine reduced it to something that was not much more than slime. When I went to inspect the combine afterwards, I found that the whole of the sieve area where the grain is divided from the chaff was covered in slime. I tried to scrape it off with a long-handled hoe but really a more effective method would have been to climb in on my hands and knees and get it off with a penknife!

The saga with the reel tines went on and on. The first set of broken reel tines were repaired under the warranty, but when the same thing happened the following season, the warranty period for the machine had expired. The new tines had their own warranty period, but Claas wouldn't honour it. I was so fed up with the combine by this point that I refused to pay the company for the new tines and was eventually summoned to the small claims court and made to explain myself. I needed to prove that tines on combine harvesters didn't normally break with that degree of regularity. So, I took with me to the court two tines from the original Matador combine harvester which was still nestling in the nettles at the back of the farm. Not one of her tines had had to be replaced in twenty-two years.

The arbitrator said that he didn't know anything about combine harvesters but he had done a spell of potato picking in his schooldays! Nevertheless, I managed to prove to him that I had not abused the machine. He found in my favour. Although I didn't have to pay for the tines,

I was told by the company supplying them that a black mark had been put against my name and that I would have a problem if I ever wanted to buy anything on hire purchase.

There were further problems with the combine. The gearbox to the main grain auger broke off and the combine broke down altogether. In the second year, the unloading auger wouldn't work. In order to buy new parts, I had to drive all the way to Wilberfoss (between York and Scarborough) to Claas's Parts' Depot. Later, the Claas Depot in Wilberfoss closed down and we had to go to Much Wenlock in Shropshire for parts. Due to all the trouble I was having with the combine, I became a regular visitor at both these places.

The instructions booklet for the combine was by now falling apart because I had flicked through it so often. We had an awful job trying to empty about four tonnes of barley out of the tank through a small slide. Then we had problems with bent rasp bars on the drum and finally with a bent 'concave' (a stone trough in front of the threshing mechanism) which we had to flatten ourselves with the help of a JCB and a sledgehammer.

It got to the stage where the Claas 106 was costing more in repairs than it was earning from contract work. I had used to enjoy harvest time as this was when you saw your reward for the year's endeavours. Now I dreaded it. Even when the combine was working, I kept wondering what was going to go wrong next. In the end, we stopped working for other people by mutual consent. We were letting them down and they were having to get other combines in to finish the job whilst we were making the repairs. We decided to struggle on just doing our own work. But the worst was yet to come.

Combine Catastrophe

In 2004, we had probably the wettest August we had ever known. The wheat was deteriorating very fast in the field. The ground was so wet that it would hardly carry a combine harvester. Farmers and contractors were fitting twin wheels and even tracks to their combines in order to be able to take their machines out in the field. Eventually, the weather came good again and we were able to start combining the wheat. The ground was all right where the drainage was good, but there were many waterlogged areas. You had to keep emptying the grain tank when it was half full to save the machine getting stuck or making some very deep ruts. In the wet places we kept coming very near to getting stuck and, in fact, in the first field that we attempted to combine, we had to leave some of the wettest parts unharvested.

I was with the combine harvester in the second field whilst my son John was over the brook loading the bales in the first field. Suddenly, without any warning, disaster struck. The combine harvester burst into flames. I was merrily driving along totally oblivious to what was going on behind me. In fact, I was thinking what an easy crop it was to harvest. Suddenly, however, I caught sight of a flame on the left hand side of the combine behind the steps up to the cab. Instinctively, I stopped and quickly reversed away from the uncut crop. I shut everything down and made a quick exit down the steps. As I did so, I grabbed a sack that I had in the cab that was usually used for wiping the windows. I had the intention of beating out the flames with it. I also grabbed my walking stick.

I soon realised that the sack was going to be useless in beating a fire of that size into submission. The flames were engulfing the whole of the centre part of the combine. The engine compartment was behind the cab over the threshing drum with the fan situated below. The fan had acted as a bellows, increasing the intensity of the fire. As I leaned on my walking stick, it became apparent that this would be the end of the combining days of the Claas 106. I also realised that I had been fortunate to get out of this situation without being badly burned. John was quickly on the scene. From the next field, he had seen smoke coming out of the machine as I was still driving along. He was very relieved to see me unharmed.

The fire brigade found the fire easily. It was a still day with the smoke going straight up into the sky. When the plastic soundproofing in the cab caught fire, it created great volumes

A sorry sight: the combine after the fire on 2 September 2004, Whitley Brook.

of smoke that could be seen for miles. Two fire engines arrived. Uncle Frank's famous words were ringing in my ears: 'She comes with a bellyful and they daren't take any home.' The fire engines remained on the road and the firemen soon had their hoses out across the field. It was not practical to go across to the combine.

The fire in the engine compartment and cab were eventually brought under control and the rest of the machine was hosed down to save some value. The grain tank caused a problem as the grain within it was smouldering and it was hard to get a hose inside. Eventually I managed to open the lids to both the engine and the grain tank with the aid of my walking stick.

Thankfully, the fire didn't ignite the swathes of straw or the uncut crop and the firemen only needed to use one engine to pump the water and one hose. The water in the second fire engine was pumped into the first fire engine supplying the hose. One of the firemen and I discussed the likely cause of the fire. He said that it had probably been a mechanical fault (such as a sealed-for-life bearing failing) or an electrical fault (such as the insulation on a wire rubbing off and causing a spark).

It was some time before the smouldering grain in the tank was extinguished. The combine looked a sorry state. It had settled at a distraught angle in ground that was now completely waterlogged. One of the large driving tyres was burnt out along with one of the steering wheels. The once proud Perkins engine was a dismal sight: the manifold and all the other components made from alloys had melted with the heat. The cab that I had loved so much was now without its glass, padding and seat upholstery. It was just a skeleton. That was the end of the 106. The parts that had not been affected were sold to a 'combine graveyard' so that they could be sold on. We were finally without a combine harvester altogether.

TWELVE

Vermin and Vacci Tankers: The Darker Side of Life on the Farm

Some people have a very romantic idea about what life is like on a farm, but the truth is very different. A lot of the work is actually dirty and very unpleasant and some of it is definitely not for the faint-hearted. As well as horses, cows and hens, there are less welcome members of the animal kingdom to contend with, including mice and rats. And as well as the pleasant activities of milking and harvesting, there are less attractive jobs such as cleaning out drains and emptying septic tanks. A great deal of my farming life has been spent dealing with the darker side of life on the farm. And, like the more pleasant side, it is has had its own challenges and rewards.

Cats

When my sister Joyce was young she got a tortoiseshell kitten as a pet. Florrie was with us many years. For a long time she was the only cat on the farm who came into the house. When Florrie had kittens, she gave birth in the hay bales. Unlike their mother, the kittens never became tame, they simply joined the rest of the cats outside on the farm. We fed them bread and milk, but they got their meat from the mice, rats and rabbits that they caught around the farmyard. Female cats will usually stop on the grounds of the farm and come to you for their food: tomcats on the other hand will roam everywhere and it's no use worrying about them. Generally speaking, the cats at Yew Tree Farm were a healthy lot, apart from when there was an occasional outbreak of cat flu. The vet once told mother that cat flu was nature's way of reducing the cat population.

After Florrie, the tortoiseshell strain remained in our cat population for many years though sometimes the colouring got rather distorted. One of Florrie's descendents, who lived on the farm after I got married, was a cat that was completely white apart from one black ear and a brown patch on one side of its face. 'Snowball', as she was called, was wild. While she was young, you couldn't get anywhere near her, let alone stroke her. When she was about ten years old, Snowball once went missing for several days. If a female cat goes missing on a farm, you start to wonder whether they are perhaps trapped behind a door that has been closed on them, or whether they are in a loft unable to get down after a ladder has been taken away. The seed potato loft at Yew Tree Farm was a particular problem in this respect as it was securely closed in winter to keep out the frost.

Snowball didn't return and we began to wonder whether she had been killed on the A50. We lost a lot of our cats as they crossed the road and, for this reason, we never attempted to control their breeding in order to keep the numbers up. Cannibal tomcats could also kill kittens. But Snowball thankfully hadn't succumbed to either of these fates. She was found, eventually, in an empty grain bin. These bins empty from the bottom, with the grain spiralling down in a cone shape. A mouse must have been on the top of the grain when the loading

Farm cats waiting to be fed.

commenced and Snowball had probably jumped in after it. We put a ladder down into the grain to get Snowball out. She didn't seem any the worse for wear but she had changed in one very significant way – she was much tamer after this and liked to come into the house. When Kathleen opened the door, she would dash straight in, up the stairs and under the bedclothes where she would snuggle up close to my daughter Margaret.

Another of our female cats once caused us some amusement. We took a load of straw which had been hanging around on the farm for several days to the local weighing station about three miles away at Winterbottom. As we were doing the weighing, this particular cat jumped out and disappeared. We didn't see her again for about three months. Female cats will often return to the farm that they are from no matter how far away they have ended up and this one was no exception. When she finally returned to Yew Tree she was pregnant. After that we had a different colour scheme in our cats for a few generations. Among them were barred grey tabbies, which are common in the Winterbottom area.

Rat Catchers

The cats were kept on the farm for a reason – to control the local rodent population. Over the years, I grew concerned that we had so many rats on the farm that the cats couldn't cope with them. None of the old methods seemed to work. To ease the problem, we started using warfarin for rodent control as soon as it became available for general use. One day, a rat catcher from the local authority called at the farm offering his services. He told me that he could offer me a contract to catch vermin for £8 a year. I checked how much the warfarin was costing me annually and together with the cost of my own time, it was far more expensive than the proposed contract, so I agreed to give it a go.

One of the rodent control men that came as a result of this contract was Bob Moore. He had been a diesel deliverer but had been made redundant. The oil company had wanted him to move to a job in sales, but this didn't appeal to him, so he applied for a job as a rat catcher with Macclesfield Borough Council. I had known Bob for a long time. He and his brother

Diamond, a farm cat, doing what she does best – catching mice.

had ferrets and they used to come round sometimes at weekends to go rabbit shooting. Bob gave my name as a reference and got the job. For a while he was worried about being made redundant again. When I asked him why, he said that the warfarin was so effective, he thought that all the rats would soon be killed off! I had to disagree with him. In my opinion, there would always be a plentiful supply of rats out in the fields and woods and along the rivers and watercourses of Cheshire.

Bob became a very accomplished pest control officer. He dealt with rats, mice, ants and wasps' nests. Mice were the hardest to control and he had to admit that keeping cats was probably the best option here. This was partly because when mice had been poisoned they usually went and found somewhere warm to lie down and die. This left a terrible smell that could be embarrassing if it was in the house. By contrast, a cat's method of killing a mouse was far more clinical.

'A Spectacular Infestation'

For many years, we had three henhouses near to each other and the hens were kept on a deep litter system. There was a wooden floor to the houses with a small space underneath – this was ideal for rats. They would go under the wooden floor, gnaw their way up into the litter (which was a lovely warm environment) and then help themselves to the food and water which was always on hand for the hens to eat. They also, of course, helped themselves to the hens.

In 1982, this problem got considerably worse. The hens would be kept for about eighteen months in the houses before they came to the end of their working life laying eggs. One of the houses contained old hens which had – as the saying goes – started 'dropping off their perches.' I had also been emptying this one particular henhouse and taking the hens to sell at Chelford Market. The first indication I had that we had a lot of rats was that as the number of hens went down, the amount of food they were consuming didn't seem to drop. With fewer hens scratching at the litter in my henhouse, a lot of rat holes started to appear and I realised that we had a major problem on our hands. If a hen died overnight, only its skeleton would be left by morning. Eventually, when I was collecting the eggs, I started to see the odd rat running about below the perches.

It was a cold winter that year with plenty of snow. Snow provides a reliable way of finding out if you have rats because their tails leave a trail behind them. The same thing happens on muddy ground. As there were no trails between the hen houses, I realised that the infestation was in one house only. It struck me that pretty soon, the rats' food supply would run out and they would have to move to another area. This was something that I wanted to avoid. I had heard stories of rats on the move after their food supply had run out. The local milkman once met a colony on the road after a load of slaughterhouse offal had been dug into the gardens at High Legh Gardens.

It was time to ask rat catcher Bob to put warfarin down under the offending henhouse. On a Friday, he put a bucketful down saying that this should be enough to last them over the weekend but by Friday evening, the whole lot had already gone and I had to ask Bob to come back. We were all very surprised by the amount that was being devoured. Over the weekend, we put down several more lots of warfarin. It wasn't until Monday that any poison at all was left in the bucket. This meant that finally, all the rats must have died.

Even then, we hadn't fully realised the enormity of the situation. We moved the muck spreader near to the henhouses and started to clean out the litter. We were in for a shock. It wasn't long before we encountered our first nest of dead rats – and there were many more to come. My son Andrew was delegated to clean out the henhouse, a job he did with great gusto, delving into the litter with a five-pronged fork and coming out with a rat on every prong. There were holes in the wooden floor and we knew that some of the litter would have gone under the floor through the holes. When we took the floorboards up, sure enough we found masses more nests of dead rats. Bob arrived with one of the lady health officers from the council to take photographs. Later, she surprised me by saying that my henhouse was regarded locally as a 'spectacular infestation.' In all we collected 130 fully grown rats. This was a complete surprise to us not least because there was no sign of rats in any other part of the farm. We were very thankful for the warfarin because without that the rat population could have spread over a very wide area.

Gamekeepers

Apart from the council rat catchers, country gamekeepers were very active in keeping the local vermin under control. They were always well respected by local farmers although they sometimes had a different interpretation of which animals ought to be classed as vermin. For example, they believed it was necessary to control the birds of prey that were responsible to some extent for killing off the small bird population.

Pheasant Shoot

We always knew when a pheasant shoot was imminent on the local estate. After the harvest, birds moved out of the woods and onto the stubble where they pecked at fallen grain. In readiness for a shoot, the gamekeeper would come along with his dogs and drive the birds back towards the woods, or at least onto land in the ownership of the estate ready for the shoot.

Farmers and gamekeepers agreed that hares were a problem. I was once combining my friend's barley on a regular basis and noticed that large patches in the middle of the field

A spectacular infestation: rats in the henhouse.

had been eaten out by what must have been a very large population of hares. In 1965, a new gamekeeper was employed on the nearby Mere Hall estate and he managed to keep reducing the number of hares until we reached a position of acceptable barley loss. He said that all the hares he had killed had tuberculosis. This gamekeeper also killed a lot of foxes. Apparently when the squire expressed concern about his control methods, the gamekeeper retorted that the squire better make his mind up whether he wanted foxes or pheasants. No more was said.

The Vacci Tanker

As well as dealing with vermin, farmers have traditionally had another unpleasant duty – moving sewage or slurry. One farmer I knew used to say that when you went into a shippon in the morning, there ought to be a barrowful of manure behind each cow. Manure is a good thing as far as farmers are concerned, but what has exercised them over the decades is how best it can be collected and redistributed over the land.

In Father's early days of farming, the machinery for moving effluent was a horse-drawn tumbril cart. The effluent was either ladled into the open-topped cart or pumped in with a chain-and-flight elevator. The tumbril cart had a seat for the operator which was in front of the container with the liquid in. As you might imagine, a steady horse was essential for emptying the cart! The valve at the back had to be operated at the same time as the vehicle was moving forward – one hand operated the valve control and the other hand held the reins. One of the hazards of this job was that if the horse didn't move off smoothly, the driver would be somersaulted backwards into the open-topped cart! Later, tractors replaced horses, but you still had to be careful.

Pretty Little Slurry

A local progressive farmer had a lagoon into which he pushed all his sewage. When it was full, he backed a low-sided trailer (or scraper) into it until the effluent filled it and slopped over the sides. His method of emptying the trailer was then to drive like hell until it all flew out across the field. Slurry in an open container needs handling very carefully as, once you get it slopping about, it is very difficult to control. One day when the lagoon was full, the tractor and scraper were driven in at speed. The slurry hit the far retaining wall and came back like a tidal wave. The tractor driver had stopped to light a cigarette. After hitting the scraper, the slurry went up in the air. It completely covered the tractor and the unsuspecting driver. It was said that afterwards the only clean part of the tractor was the driver's seat after he had dismounted!

Necessity is the mother of invention. With increasing amounts of farm effluent, a machine was developed in the 1970s known as a Vacci tanker. This had the ability to fill itself and to discharge its own contents. There was just one lever: pushed one way it created a vacuum in the tank which allowed the effluent to be sucked in through a pipe. If you pushed the lever the other way, it created pressure to blow the effluent out. Needless to say, you had to be very careful which way you pushed the lever! Having a Vacci tank on pressure rather than vacuum could potentially have disastrous results.

When I got the Vacci tanker at Yew Tree Farm in about 1976, my first job was to empty our recently constructed effluent tank. Some newly turned out calves came to inspect the whole operation from behind a barbed wire fence. The six-inch plastic pipe from the tanker was very stiff and needed a lot of bending to get it into the effluent tank. I must have interpreted the

The Vacci tanker discharging its load. On a sunny day if the effluent is fairly clear, all the colours of the rainbow are visible.

instructions wrongly. I put the tanker under pressure. This wouldn't have been too disastrous if the pipe had behaved itself. What should have happened is that a rush of air should have entered the effluent, just stirring it. In fact, the pipe came out of the tank with a sudden rush of air. The calves were startled and were soon at the opposite end of the field. I had to be thankful: it would have been a lot worse if the tanker had already sucked in some effluent.

As the laws on pollution became more stringent, the Vacci tanker was in greater and greater demand on neighbouring farms. One evening, my cousin, Jim Wright, phoned. He was concerned that his silage effluent tank would overflow and possibly get into a watercourse feeding a local lake. There had already been trouble with the owners of the lake resulting in Jim being prosecuted and he was particularly anxious that it shouldn't happen again. He also wanted me to have a look at a septic tank belonging to a man named Jerry who worked for him. It was the first time I had been asked to clean out a septic tank.

I had read up on the Vacci machine's instructions the night before and had noted some useful advice. According to the booklet, if when cleaning out a tank you encountered a solid mass with some liquid, the stuff should be mixed thoroughly before it was sucked into the tanker. When I arrived at Jerry's, he directed me to a field behind his cottage and told me to back up to a very tall hedge. He went on the other side of the hedge and it was apparent that he had taken the concrete flag off the top of the septic tank ready for the pipe to go in. I obeyed the instruction book and decided to stir the tank first. I put the tanker shaft in gear and opened the valve. From the resulting noise, I realised immediately that everything was not going to plan. I turned everything off and crawled under the hedge to see Jerry wiping his face with his hands and taking off his overalls, which were covered in sewage! To me it was a hysterical situation, but Jerry was not amused and told me it was nothing to laugh at. In my opinion, the instruction book to the Vacci tanker has got it wrong. If you blow air into a full tank, sewage can be blown out over the surrounding area with disastrous consequences.

When people find out that you are able to clean out septic tanks, you become everybody's friend. When they find out their toilets aren't functioning properly, your company and that of your Vacci tanker is requested as soon as possible. I have, for instance, often been called out to sort out the Port-a-loos at events at local stately homes. At one such event, I made a grand entrance through the main gates – it was the only way in. My evangelical acquaintance John Pennington was there with his banner which read, 'Jesus Saves'. We agreed that we were there on different but related missions: he was looking after the spiritual needs of the people and I was attending to their material needs! I asked John whether he thought that there would be any need for a Vacci tanker in heaven. He said that he didn't think so, as there were no material needs there!

One event I used to attend with the Vacci tanker was the Medieval Fair at a local stately home. People were dressed up in suits of armour and chain mail, walking about with huge swords and balls and chains. Every so often they would square up to each other and have a pretend fight. I wondered why these medieval characters had any need of Port-a-loos at all. Why didn't they just nippeth behind a tree as they had done in days of old?

Sometimes, some rather unusual objects have blocked the pipe of the Vacci tanker. An object may be sucked in through the wide suction hose but may be too large to be blown out again through the smaller spray orifice. Suddenly, the effluent stops coming out, and the pressure starts building up in the tank. Everything has to be shut off and the pressure eliminated from the tank. Retrieving the article causing the blockage can be a delicate operation because, wherever the object is, there will still be pressure. Whether you poke a bar at the obstruction or unclasp the offending section of pipe, you are very likely to get a shot of slurry. On one occasion, I had been cleaning out a septic tank for my friend J.P. It was full of a thick gluey sort of slurry and the Vacci pump was very sluggish in its operations. I later found out that a brick had become wedged inside the suction hose.

An Unusual Blockage

I was once asked to help clean out the goldfish pond at one of the local big houses. The family helped out by netting the fish beforehand. The pond was lined with concrete, so we had the satisfaction of a clean finish. The last load would contain the thickest sludge and any articles that had found their way into the pond. It soon became apparent that there was an obstruction in the Vacci tanker. I went through the usual procedure and to my surprise found a goldfish held by the tail at the shut off valve. I couldn't retrieve it without cutting its tail off!

One of the most satisfying jobs I ever did with the Vacci Tanker was in my capacity as local councillor. I received a phone call from a very disillusioned elector who said that he had been given my name by another councillor from Styal. The elector had a problem: after a heavy thunderstorm, the patio at the rear of his house and the drive at the front of his house had become submerged in sewage. When he had told the councillor the nature of his problem, the chap had said, 'You appear to be in the sh★t. I can't think of anybody better than Walter Wright to get you out of it.'

The elector seemed to just want to make me aware of his predicament more than anything else. But I decided that I could probably help. I called round at his house in Mere the next morning to find plenty of yellow vehicles with flashing lights. The men from the council appeared to have been on site some time, but couldn't get their machinery to work. I backed the tanker down the drive, selected a suitable grid on the lowest part of the drive, put the pipe down and left the rest to tractor and tanker. Very soon, the tide of sewage was going down. Two council men with brushes soon cleaned up the debris that had been left behind.

As I was tying the pipe back to the tanker, an official-looking person wearing a hard hat and carrying a clipboard came up and asked me who I was. I said with great pride that I was the local councillor. I don't think that I have ever seen a look of astonishment on anybody's face to match his!

I went back later that day to see if everything had been sorted out and found that the council men had left without clearing the drains. They had continued to be unable to get their machinery to work. The Vacci tank was empty again by now and had an appetite for more sewage. As I have always done, I just got on and completed the job.

THIRTEEN

Farmer in Court and the Rise of a New Generation

In November 1984, there was a particularly unfortunate incident at Yew Tree Farm. This story is a lesson in what can go wrong on a farm and how important it is for those who work on farms to take proper precautions at all times. It is also a tale about how the little man – and a farmer at that – can end up taking on the might of the law.

Accident at the Farm

It all came about because we decided to build a workshop to help us repair cars and farm machinery. The workshop was largely the idea of my two boys, John and Andrew. They were very different. John was interested in farming, especially milking cows, but was not as accomplished as far as mending machinery went. He had successfully attended an O.N.D. course at Reascheath Agricultural College. Andrew, on the other hand, hated cattle and, from when he was very young, told his mother that he wanted the cows 'willing' to John. He had also been to Reaseheath College but took an agricultural engineering course, building anything on wheels that would go fast, especially off road. Andrew was very much involved with the digging side of the farm business and spent his spare time renovating cars, buying crashed vehicles, and repairing them or transferring all the reusable parts – engine, gearbox, seats, etc – into other body shells. My daughter Margaret was the academic of the family. She studied architecture and eventually became an architect.

Our repair facilities at Yew Tree Farm were very crude, with most of the repairs being done outside, or in one of the sheds if it was available. The need for a workshop increased as the farm became more mechanised and as our expertise developed with Andrew's growing engineering knowledge. We all decided that it would be a good idea to build the workshop in the farmyard. It should have doors that could be closed to keep the elements out and be high enough to take a trailer and large enough to take most farm implements. It was clear also that we would need an inspection pit to service road vehicles.

The End of an Era

The first thing we did when we decided to build the workshop was to demolish some old buildings in the farmyard including the outside privy. This was a place where I am sure many big decisions about the farm had been made over the years and I was sorry to see it go!

A recognised shed building firm came and built the workshop, incorporating a track for an overhead chain hoist. We were to concrete the lower walls and floor ourselves. At first, we

Above: Work at Yew Tree Farm has always been a partnership between man and machine.

Left: The scene of the accident: the workshop at Yew Tree Farm.

thought that a pit of about 4ft deep would suffice for the inspection pit. When we realised that it would have to be 5.5ft deep, I was concerned. I knew that the area in which we had to dig was built on a sand and gravel bank and that we would have to be very careful. I had experienced a similar problem when digging out a pit for our grain store. The sides on that occasion had been sloped to forty-five degrees to improve safety.

The sides of the inspection pit had to be vertical and, I knew, there was danger of the sides slipping whilst they were being excavated. We had encountered this hazard when laying deep drains, so we knew what we had to take into account. In those cases, we knew that we must either dig the trench wider at the top so that it had sloped sides or use shuttering to support the sides whilst we laid pipes in the bottom. I thought through all the precautions we had to take and we began to dig the pit in early November. Andrew worked the excavator, driving forward into the building, scooping up a bucket of spoil, backing out, swinging and emptying it into a trailer. I was keeping the sides vertical with a spade and measuring all the correct dimensions. Our helper David Okell was assisting me with the tape measure. He was usually the excavator driver and had little experience of working in a trench.

On the 6 November, we had almost finished the excavation and there was a small amount of loose soil that needed shovelling into the excavator by hand. This is when disaster struck. A small amount of soil fell off the side of the pit. It must have startled David, who swung around and suddenly collapsed on the floor in severe pain. There was no mistaking his predicament as his foot must have stuck in the wet sand at the bottom of the pit and was at the wrong angle to his leg. When his body twisted, his leg bones must have snapped.

We sent for the ambulance and made David as comfortable as possible. The most distressing part was lifting him out of the trench because he was in a great deal of pain. This was a very serious situation. We had a legal responsibility towards David and I contacted Health and Safety straight away. He was taken to Warrington hospital and his leg was X-rayed and set. He was soon home and moving around on crutches. As he lived with his elderly mother and was the only driver in the family, his situation caused him problems for some time. We all visited him on a regular basis and took him the daily newspapers.

I had Employer's Liability Insurance and thought that this would cover the situation, but it was not going to be that easy. Our local Health and Safety officer visited all farms in the area that employed workers and advised the farmers on how to keep the place safe. Usually, we farmers accepted the wisdom of the safety officers (though I am not saying we welcomed them with open arms). Most of the regulations brought in by Health and Safety were the result of rare serious or fatal accidents. In many cases, the farmer responsible had become complacent and had not noticed the deterioration of his machinery. We knew that we had to comply with the recommendations and we did.

Whilst David was recovering, John, Andrew and I finished digging out the pit and made up the shuttering to form the shape of an inspection pit. We then started to pour in the concrete. Apart from some of the steps down into the pit, the concreting job was completed before the Health and Safety officer came to visit us on 12 December 1984, over a month after the accident took place. He asked me some questions and took a photograph of the inspection pit. He then went to see David to get a statement from him. Returning to the farm a few days later, he said that he thought that there were grounds to take out a prosecution against me for carrying out unsafe practices, but that the ultimate decision rested with his superior. I was furious, knowing just how careful we had been and believing the accident to have been unavoidable. On 24 January 1984, I had confirmation from Health and Safety that they were indeed going to prosecute me and that I would get the necessary summons in due course. My insurance company took legal advice regarding the claim and once they heard that Health and Safety had decided to prosecute, they said it was an open-and-shut case and wouldn't pay the legal costs to allow me to defend the case. The general opinion is in these situations was that you should plead guilty. The Farmers' Union representative, Robin Jones, who would represent David, and had found him a solicitor, came round to break the news: 'Will you plead guilty?' he asked.

'Shall I hell as like,' I replied.

'I thought you'd say that,' he said.

   Over the course of my life I had had few encounters with the law (apart from a few local drainage issues where I was in dispute with neighbouring farmers and my battle with the manufacturers of my combine harvester). I was very apprehensive about appearing even before a magistrate and the thought of appearing before a judge and jury in the Crown Court scared me to death. I was also worried about the cost of a barrister. Nevertheless, this was a matter of principle and I was determined to fight my corner.

Case in the Magistrates' Court

The course of justice moves very slowly. I received my summons to appear at the Magistrates' Court in Knutsford in August (nine months after the accident had occurred). As I was pleading not guilty, I didn't need to turn up in person, I was simply advised of the date of the next hearing. I was then called to the Magistrates' Court in October for the committal for trial. This is when things started to get complicated. As I was waiting to be called, the clerk to the court informed me that the Health and Safety officer hadn't turned up and that I might as well go home. Apparently, without both parties being present, the committal couldn't take place. I was a bit concerned about going home just on the authority of the clerk of the court and I asked a policeman who was standing nearby to be a witness to what had been said.

   By the time of my next appearance in court on 20 November (more than a year after the accident), I had been made aware of the case for the prosecution and had seen David's statement and the statement from the Health and Safety officer. The summons this time implied that the committal for trial had taken place the last time that I was at the court. This, of course, was not the case.

   I was escorted to the dock and was asked to confirm my name and my plea of 'not guilty.' As the magistrate asked the clerk to the court to outline the case, I realised with horror that the trial itself was getting under way. This, I knew, was not how it should be, so I intervened, making a representation to the magistrate. I said that I didn't think we could start the trial that day as we had not yet had the committal. I pointed out that I had been sent home on my last visit to the court.

   Magistrates may be used to solicitors intervening in the protocol of the court but not to farmers questioning the legality of trials. The three people on the bench looked startled and the court was thrown into turmoil. The magistrates retired to consider their position and were absent for at least fifteen minutes. When they returned, they agreed that the committal had not taken place, but said that the Health and Safety people had been in the building at the time of my last visit and that I should not have been asked to leave.

   They concluded that as I had already received the necessary information about the trial, it should go ahead. One of the magistrates asked me if I had any witnesses that I would be calling. I said I had two witnesses but I had not brought them with me as I had been under the impression that the trial would not go ahead. I felt that the magistrates were covering up for the inefficiencies in the way the court was being run. I stuck to my guns and said that we had not had the committal for the trial and on the basis of that I had not brought my witnesses along with me. I insisted that we could not go ahead with the trial.

   I was worried now that even if the magistrates agreed to a deferral, I might have blotted my copybook sufficiently to mean that I would not get a fair trial. The magistrate said in a very stern voice that they proposed to go ahead with the trial and if I didn't agree, the only option was for me to elect to be tried by a judge and jury in the Crown Court. I realised this was the only way to go, so I agreed. The magistrate asked me if I had anybody to represent me in court and that if I hadn't I would be very well advised to get somebody. I told him I hadn't and that his suggestion was a matter of opinion.

There was quite some time before the trial and I had a lot of thinking to do. My friends in the farming community told me that if Health and Safety had decided to prosecute, there wasn't much chance of getting a non-guilty verdict. I needed to decide whether or not I needed a barrister to represent me – I actually wondered whether anyone would take me on. I also realised that I had developed into a do-it-yourself type over the years. On the farm we had improvised by doing jobs like drainage works, making farm trailers, pouring concrete walls, making our own grain bins and installing grain-handling equipment. But whether or not I was up to defending myself in a Crown Court was another matter. I decided, however, that I would give it a try.

There followed several months of quiet preparation on my part. I had received a brief from the prosecution containing the grounds for prosecution and David's statement about what had happened. I had asked the Health and Safety officer whether or not he wanted statements from John and Andrew and he said he didn't. The court knew that I would be challenging the prosecution case, but apart from my own statement to Health and Safety and my plea of 'not guilty,' nobody knew anything about how I would mount my defence. I simply indicated that I would be calling John and Andrew as witnesses.

I read the case for the prosecution many times. In essence, it argued that the accident had been caused by my negligence and that the walls of the inspection pit had completely collapsed and damaged David's leg. I got more and more depressed every time I read the case, not because I thought it was accurate, but because I wondered whether or not I had the evidence to contradict it. People said that I was very quiet the day before the trial.

The Flaw in the Case

It was only a few days before the trial that I realised that there was a flaw in the Health and Safety officer's report. It said that the ground conditions in the pit had been very unstable and, because of the type of subsoil and water, the walls had been liable to collapse at any time. I suddenly remembered that the Health and Safety officer had taken so long in coming to visit us that he had not actually seen the pit before it was concreted. The day that he visited, the only part of the pit that was not concreted was one of the steps – and the subsoil on this was perfectly dry. At last I had found something on which to base my case.

Case in the Crown Court

The day of the trial dawned. I didn't want Kathleen to attend the court because I was afraid of making a fool of myself in front of her, but I was accompanied by Andrew and John, so it was quite a family affair. David, now back working for us after ten months' absence whilst his leg healed, was chief witness for the prosecution.

The atmosphere in the Crown Court in Knutsford was quite forbidding. The judge stated that this was an unusual trial as prosecutions by Health and Safety were usually tried in a Magistrates' Court. He said that the Crown Court had been my choice so we had better get on with it. By the tone of his voice, I gathered that he felt that a case like this was rather too trivial for him to be involved in. He then asked the barrister for the prosecution whether the two sides had found any common ground. On being told that we hadn't, he asked that we retire to see if we could find some.

We were ushered into a small room. To my surprise, the barrister for the prosecution came straight out and said, 'You're guilty aren't you?' I retorted with some anger that I was certainly not guilty and that this was what we were here for. It was up to the court to decide. There was a third person in the room whose identity I had not been told. When I asked who he was, I discovered he was the supporting solicitor for the prosecution. I was becoming increasingly

The scene of the challenge: Knutsford Crown Court.

annoyed about the way I was being treated. It started to dawn on me that many people who take a case to the Crown Court change their plea on arrival – probably, it seemed to me, because of intimidation. Well, it wasn't going to happen to me. I was even more determined to put my case than ever before. An old saying kept going through my mind, 'Never let it be said that your mother bred a jibber.'

The Health and Safety officer was the first witness for the prosecution. He was asked his qualifications and I was interested to find out that he had been to agricultural college. This confirmed my belief that he knew a lot about agriculture from a theoretical point of view, but probably not from a practical point of view. The prosecution continued to question him and outlined the prosecution case that we had been working in unstable conditions and had not taken the necessary precautions to avoid an accident.

It was now my turn to question him. I can't say that I despised him: I had got along with him very well over the years and I realised that I could have been faced with a far more vindictive opponent. However, this was not the time for niceties. If I was to be prosecuted, I was in for a hefty fine with costs awarded to the prosecution. I began my questioning by asking him if he had been concerned about standards of safety at Yew Tree Farm in the past. I thought I was on to a safe bet with this question as he had said before that he had always previously been satisfied with my safety standards. He agreed that he had.

I decided then that it was time to get a bit more aggressive. I questioned him about the timing of his first visit to the farm after the accident. The accident had happened on 6 November and he had turned up on 12 December. I suggested that through incompetence he had not inspected the scene of the accident as soon as it was reported. He replied that he had been under a lot of work pressure. This led me on to my next question about the condition of the ground being unstable. He replied that it had been. This was when I went in for the kill. I reminded him that when he visited on 12 December, the pit was concreted apart from one step that had given no signs of being unstable. He had to agree, rather sheepishly, that he had not seen the pit before it was concreted, but had only presumed it was unstable.

The prosecution then called David Okell and asked him questions about the accident and about the fall of soil. David said that he had been startled by the soil falling but that everything had happened so quickly, he couldn't say exactly how it had happened.

It was now my turn to cross-examine David. We established how long we had worked together and how David was usually the excavator driver whilst I usually worked in the trench. He agreed that over the years, we had dug much deeper trenches together than the one in the inspection pit and that we had either made the trench in a V- shape to stop the sides slipping in, or used shuttering to ensure safe working conditions. David confirmed that we had always practised safe working conditions and that he had not been concerned when he followed me into the pit on the day of the accident.

A Vital Piece of Evidence

I had to dispel the prosecution's theory that the sides of the pit had totally collapsed, thus causing David's leg to break. Rather than producing documentary evidence from a briefcase as a barrister would have done, I reached into a plastic supermarket carrier bag that I had brought with me. My evidence consisted of my farm diary and a few pieces of paper with a timetable of the events written on them, a list of the questions that I was asking, a tape measure, and a photo of the building and pit. I pulled out one last object – a Wellington boot!

I lifted the boot aloft so that it could be seen by the judge and members of the jury. There was a gasp of surprise. Fortunately, I had taken the precaution of washing the boot after that morning's milking. I asked David if he could confirm that he had been wearing a similar Wellington on the day of the accident. I went on to establish how deep the fall of soil had been. We agreed that it had only covered his foot and that his foot was not stuck 'fast' in the soil when we moved him out of the pit. What I was trying to establish was that there had not

The evidence – a boot and a plastic bag.

been a major collapse of the walls in the way that the prosecution was trying to claim. My final question to David was to ask him whether or not he had suffered financially as a result of the accident. He replied that he hadn't.

The Usher's Tale

My sons were not allowed into the courtroom until they gave evidence. Whilst they waited outside, they got talking to the court usher who had worked on a farm in Mobberley. Before he knew who they were, he started telling them about the very amusing trial that was currently going on in court, in which a farmer who was defending himself had produced a Wellington boot as evidence!

The next day, it was my turn to give my own statement of defence. I spoke of my twenty-three years experience of digging trenches and drainage work. When you are in court, it is not the time for modesty: I had to claim that I was near perfect and didn't make mistakes. In a lot of people's eyes, I am probably a bumbling old fool, but the last thing I had to do at that point was to admit it. I told the court that the building above the pit had been erected in March and that the area being dug out – far from being wet as the prosecution had claimed – was in fact dry since it had been under cover for many months. The building even had doors on to stop the rain blowing in.

My son John was my first witness. I had great pleasure in introducing him. I asked him to tell the court his agricultural qualifications, knowing that they were better than those of the safety officer. I asked John lots of questions: the position of David in the pit in relation to where the soil had fallen in, the depth of the soil around his foot, how we had eased David's foot out of the soil and what depth it was. I asked him to explain how we had carefully planned the whole operation. He described how the pit was to be dug to a depth of 4ft 3in – although the finished depth would be greater because of the raised floor level. John spoke with clarity and confidence; he was a practical person with a good education and was not overawed by the situation.

The barrister for the prosecution, in his cross-examination, asked John about his education. He wanted to know whether land drainage had been part of the curriculum. John replied that it had and that he had been made aware of the problems connected with it. The lawyer put it to John that the sides of the pit had entirely collapsed. John denied it. I was allowed to come back after the prosecution's cross-examination. I asked John to confirm that it was just a bit of soil that fell in and not a total collapse.

My son Andrew was my other witness. I asked him to describe the planning before we started digging the pit. Andrew explained that he had been frustrated that we could not start digging the pit earlier and said that I had held him back so that I could plan the safety aspects. We also discussed how he had dug the pit through the open doorway with a 360 degree type excavator with a long reach. Andrew explained how he drove the excavator up to the door of the building (so that its tracks were outside the building), scooped up a bucket of soil, reversed back until he could swing the bucket and deposited the soil in a trailer. The fact that the excavator was outside the building meant that it was less likely to have caused the area around the pit to vibrate. We had done everything possible to ensure that there was minimum stress on the sides of the pit and thus to reduce the chances of a collapse.

I then had to take to the witness box whilst the prosecution examined me. I just did my best and hoped that the jury would have mercy on me. As time went on, the barrister for the prosecution seemed to be asking questions of me which had no connection with the charge. He kept suggesting digging scenarios totally unlike the drainage or digging jobs with which I was familiar. I suppose he was using his skills of cross-examination to prove my incompetence. But I was getting fed up with his questions. Finally, when he asked me a question that I thought was totally irrelevant, I said, 'Sir, you are in the realms of fantasy'. This marked the end of the questioning.

The judge then gave his summing up of the case bringing forward the main points made by both parties. I must say that he gave a fair summing up of the evidence and highlighted an important part of my defence about the fact that (at that depth), if a trench does not collapse as the excavator is digging it, then there would be a time lapse before it did collapse. The judge then closed the case for evidence and the jury retired to consider their verdict.

The Verdict

The jury were out for about an hour. The judge had two cases running concurrently and I became very engrossed in listening from the public gallery to the other case — a burglary. When there was a break, we were recalled. The foreman of the jury reported that they had not reached a unanimous verdict and that they were split, ten to two. The judge ordered them back to try to reach a unanimous verdict. This was the worst part for me. I knew that the jury were divided, but I didn't know which way. After this, my thoughts were all with the jury and I could no longer get interested in the other case.

At last the judge reassembled the court and asked again for the foreman of the jury's verdict. Much to my relief and surprise, the foreman said 'not guilty.'

The judge dismissed the jury and the ordeal was over.

In the car park outside the court, three members of the jury came up to me. One said that he had come all the way from Bollington to look after me. The second said that what had saved me was the fact that I had paid David's wages whilst he was off work. This hadn't been mentioned directly in court, but I had alluded to it when I had asked David if he had suffered in any way financially. The third one said, 'If you ever do anything like this again, get that son of yours to defend you. He's better than you'.

Prepared for the verdict on the steps of the court.

It was only then that we noticed the Health and Safety officer trying to start his car. The battery was flat and a push was needed. The farm hands soon had the car started. It was no use holding a grudge.

As we drove home we were all in good spirits. I reflected on how even the barrister for the prosecution had come over and congratulated me at the end. We had both said that there were no hard feelings. In fact, I felt a bit sorry for him. I don't think he could understand how a person who worked with a spade at the bottom of a trench for a living could have taken on the might of the system and won!

A New Generation

Although they were very different, my three children liked to help each other out and occasionally, there were events in the locality that brought them all together. In the mid 1980s, when he was in his early twenties, John had followed in my footsteps and become chairman of the Knutsford Young Farmers' Club. The ethics of the YFC was still the same as it had been in my day, with a great deal of effort being put in to raising money for charity.

The club had the idea of doing a charity bicycle ride from Knutsford to Blackpool to raise money for the Knutsford Ambulance Station. My boys wanted this to be a bike ride with a difference and soon plans were afoot. I noticed that there suddenly seemed to be a lot of activity in the workshop on the farm. For years, Andrew and his friend Austen had been building self-propelled machines called 'doon buggies' which they raced around the stubble fields after harvest. These were well-built vehicles with safety frames, but their object was speed. Both Andrew and Austen had ended up with a lot bruises and some broken limbs over the years.

I wondered what invention the boys had dreamed up this time. My presence in the workshop was not always appreciated and my sons tended to work on the principle that 'what the eye doesn't see, the heart doesn't grieve over.' Usually the doors of the workshop were kept tightly closed, except when I occasionally exerted my authority and said that they must make room for tractors and farm machinery. I had always been a nut-and-bolt man and had graduated from building Meccano as a child to building trailers for use on the farm. However, I didn't have the feel for creating new designs that Andrew and Austen had. Eventually, curiosity got the better of me and I took a peep through the doors of the workshop. I spotted some long lengths of box steel but little else.

What, in fact, was being built in the workshop this time was not another doon buggy, but a vehicle that would have a lot slower propulsion, seats, pedals and a handlebars. The boys were building a magnificent bike for the charity ride. The final design was quite incredible: an eighteen-seater bike (with two lines of nine seats). Andrew and Austen made many trips to the council tip to cannabilise old bicycles for parts; other bits and pieces were donated by friends (the steel, for example, was from my old friend Trundle who built farm sheds). 'Daisy,' as the bicycle became known, had a Vauxhall Viva front axle for the steering and brakes. This would be controlled by Andrew who would ride at the front. The chains met centrally in an Escort gearbox so that there was nearly equal pressure on all the chains. The back axle was from a Ford Cortina. All the riders would have a seat and handlebars, and everyone would supply horsepower through the pedals.

One Sunday evening, I was just settling down to watch a good programme on television when the boys asked if I would come and help trial the machine on its maiden voyage. I climbed aboard with a certain degree of trepidation: it certainly wasn't a speed trial as there were only four of us providing the energy on this occasion. The slope up from the workshop to the gates onto the A50 road is quite steep and it was an effort to get Daisy up there. Aware of the poor visibility on the bend, we turned left and then immediately right into Wrenshot Lane and made excellent progress until we came level with the large gates of a local millionaire's house. Andrew had decided that this was an appropriate place to try to turn

Daisy, the bicycle
made for eighteen.

round. I was sceptical: the bike was 24ft long, and manoeuvrability was obviously going to be quite a problem. The need to be able to reverse was essential: those peddling would have to be able to synchronise. Andrew instructed us to stop peddling: he applied the brakes and Austen engaged reverse gear. As we resumed pedalling, I was amazed to see that the bike did indeed go backwards. We accomplished a three-point turn and headed back to Yew Tree Farm.

A Bike with Style

Gradually the eighteen-seater bike was fitted out with lights, a flashing light for safety, a radio and even a cigarette lighter for the benefit of a lad called Eric who would ride on the back row and who was a compulsive smoker!

There were some mechanical problems over the next few weeks, of course. At one point, the chains all had to be renewed with stronger ones which were kindly donated by John Wright and Sons. The other problem was that the pedals and cranks had been taken from ordinary bicycles and weren't terribly robust. There wasn't much we could do about this. Tandem pedals (which would have been stronger) were – as they say – 'harder to come by than rocking horse manure on a waste disposal site!'

I never rode the bike again, but I watched with great interest as it was fitted out to meet the needs and comforts of its future riders. Over the coming weeks, Andrew and his friends made many trips out on a Sunday night to synchronise the people power, and iron out any faults. Invariably they all ended up in one of the local pubs. 'Daisy' was also soon making the rounds of various local events. She was put on view at the annual rally at Reaseheath College and then at the Cheshire show where she created considerable interest amongst the general public outside the tent of the Young Farmers' Club.

The bike ride to Blackpool finally took place on a Saturday in June 1987. For once my three children were involved in doing something together. My son John had been chairman of the Knutsford Young Farmer's Club the previous year but the ride and the funds it raised would fall under his period of office. Andrew was in charge of the whole business, and my daughter Margaret also took part – riding some of the way and also acting as an 'outrider' escorting the bike.

The night before the ride, the cyclists socialised for a while together in the Kilton Pub, but the next morning, they were up and off early, setting off from Knutsford Ambulance Station

It was a great moment when the finish line was reached.

at about 8 a.m. The money raised would eventually be used to train the ambulance personnel there in using defibrillators. Daisy was followed by a support vehicle that included a portable welder just in case any repairs needed to be done to the bike en route. A number of extra cyclists on their own bicycles acted as outriders.

It had turned out to be a very wet summer and this particular June day was no exception, with the rain falling incessantly all the way to Blackpool. Andrew issued orders all the way like an old washerwoman. In fact, he gained the nickname 'Washer' from this trip and it has stuck with him ever since. It wasn't long before the riders needed a comfort break. Twenty-five cold and wet people poured simultaneously into the Little Chef at Preston, much to the dismay of the staff.

The team finally arrived in Blackpool wet and bedraggled at 6 p.m. Young Farmers' have thrift instilled into them. Once they reached Blackpool, not for them the Imperial or the Metropol hotels, not even a bed and breakfast: instead they slept in a church hall. Some of the parents of the cyclists had driven to Blackpool in their cars and had brought sleeping bags. The church hall also provided somewhere for the cyclists' wet clothes to dry out. The food had been prepared in advance by Kathleen, Tom Goostrey (the club president) and his wife Betty. Kathleen took the food to Blackpool with the club treasurer, John Royle, Kathryn Whitlow and other parents on the Saturday and then came home again. The food was much relished by those weary riders. How much sleep they got in the church hall, I don't know. Once they were trussed up in their sleeping bags, they apparently started having 'maggot' races around the floor!

The following day, it was bright and sunny. The riders' clothes had dried out and their spirits were high. They pedalled Daisy along the seafront where they were given a rapturous welcome by the crowds. Kathleen and John went up again to see them off. On the way home, the party accompanying the bike in the van waited in the same Little Chef for the fundraisers to arrive. When they appeared, there was a cry from the staff, 'We're not having them in here – we haven't cleaned up from yesterday yet.'

After a short breakdown when a pedal needed welding by the backup team, Daisy arrived back at Knutsford Ambulance Station at about 8.30 p.m. on Sunday evening with a tired but happy crew. They had raised £4,500 for a very good cause. This called for a celebration and what better place to have it than our local pub, the Kilton?

The bicycle ride to Blackpool pulled together all our family's skills and strengthened our links with the local community and the Young Farmers' Federation. It was one of our happiest times.

Postscript

The Cheshire countryside looks very different today from how it did when I was a child. In general, there are fewer and bigger farms and larger machines. Many local buildings that were farms have been tastefully converted into homes, or second homes. There have also been enormous changes in what is farmed and how much is produced.

In the 1950s, there were twenty-seven farmers milking cows in the High Legh area: today, in 2007, there are just two. The Milk Marketing Board was abolished in 1994 to meet the requirements of a free market and since then it seems that milk buyers have only been interested in economies of scale. One buyer for Sainsbury's remarked recently that he isn't interested in farmers – he wants to buy from businessmen who are prepared to keep very large herds of cows. At Yew Tree Farm today, my son John has seventy milking cows. Other farmers are operating herds of over a thousand milking cows over several sites.

Many local farmers are renting out their land to growers of grain and potatoes. Specialist potato growers can individually harvest up to 450 acres. In co-operation with other growers, they then market their produce to multi-national crisping companies. These growers have all the latest harvesting equipment, grading and storage facilities in which the heating and humidity is controlled. All this is to ensure that the final product is a perfect crisp. We have come a long way since Irish workers were 'paid by the score' to dig up potatoes with a fork!

Somewhat surprisingly to me, in Cheshire, at least, there seems to be no unemployment among farmers. Many farmers' sons and farm workers have diversified into other related occupations: gardening and landscape work (using their excavators), providing fencing for horses and riding establishments and even working on barn conversions. There are also more places growing flowers and salad vegetables. These were traditionally produced closer to Manchester, but as the conurbation has grown, businesses have been relocated into our area.

All these changes have affected the relationships between farmers, farm workers and other people who live and work in the countryside. There is less time to get to know people, less time, perhaps, to study character and enjoy the humour. But, some things, I am glad to say, haven't changed. My son John still farms the 200 acres connected with Yew Tree Farm on his own, apart from on those occasions when he needs extra help. He is the only farmer in Mere growing potatoes and David Pimlott, the son of my old friend J.P., is the only farmer in High Legh doing the same. The old rivalry that I had with his father is still there. John and David still compete to see who can pick the first early potatoes. And what's more, I'm proud to say, that both of them still plant their potatoes in manure, just as their fathers did!

Yew Tree Farm as it is today – some things have changed but a lot remains the same.

Winnie, the Foster Traction Engine that drove the threshing machine at Yew Tree Farm. Today she appears regularly at steam shows.